GB's Café

Other books by Ginna BB Gordon

Bear Me Away to Another World
The tale of a duo, the power of music, and a chandelier
A novel by Ginna BB Gordon with David Gordon

The Soup Kit
A comprehensive map for creating good soups from scratch

The Lavandula Series
Novels based on the fictional journals of Stefani Michel

Book One: *Looking for John Steinbeck*

Book Two: *Deke Interrupted*

Book Three: *Humming in Spanish*

The Honey Baby Darlin' Series
A serial memoir about cooking, love, & the love of cooking

Book One: *Bonnebrook*

Book Two: *The Gingerbread Farm*

Sunny Mae & Bird in Alaska
A read-aloud book with illustrations by Dai Thomas

First You Grow the Pumpkin
100 Cool Things to Make and Preserve

A Simple Celebration
The Nutritional Program from the Chopra Center for Well Being
Written as Ginna Bell Bragg, with David Simon, MD
Foreword by Deepak Chopra (pub. by Random House)

the bakery

Ginna BB Gordon

Lucky Valley Press
Pacific Grove, California

Copyright © 2025 by Ginna BB Gordon

Published by Lucky Valley Press
Pacific Grove, California

ISBN: 979-8-218-58690-4

All rights reserved. This book and its contents are protected under International and Federal Copyright Laws and Treaties. Except for the quotation of short passages for the purpose of criticism or review, no part of this book may be reproduced or transmitted in any form or by any means, electronic or mechanical, including photocopying, recording, or by any information storage and retrieval system, without express written permission from the author.

Cover photo and all illustrations by the author
Photos from the author's collection

Book design by Lucky Valley Press
Pacific Grove, California
www.luckyvalleypress.com

Printed on acid-free paper

Contents

To Be a Baker ix
Sugar and Alternatives xi

Breakfast & Brunch

Baked Orange French Toast 3
Cottage Cheese Pancakes. 4
Dates with Cheesecake Filling 4
Legendary Cream Scones 5
World's Greatest Pancakes. 7
Granola Two Ways 8
Apple Fritters 10

Quick Bread & Muffins

Irish Soda Bread 12
Cranberry Bread 13
Cloud Biscuits 14
Date Bread. 15
Blue Cornbread 16
Buttermilk Muffins 17
Crumb Topping 18

Yeast & Sourdough Breads

Basic Sourdough Bread 20
Sourdough Cinnamon Rolls 22
English Muffins. 26
French Bread. 28
Oatmeal Bread 29
Cinnamon Rolls. 30
Swedish Tea Ring 32
Hot Cross Buns 33
Golden Crescents 34
Cheese Straws 35
Sour Cream Buns. 36
60 Minute Sweet Dough 37

Cinnamon Swirls 38
Pecan Roll. 38
Glazed Donuts 39
Croissants. 41

Savory Flatbreads, Crackers & Pizza

Pizza Dough. 46
Down Home Corn-Spoon 47
Scottish Oat Cakes 48
Chapatis 49
Tortillas. 50
Sourdough Crackers. 51
Cornish Pasties. 54
Shortcrust Pastry. 55
Vegetable Pot Pie. 56
Savory Crumb Topping 56
Pastry Dough for Vegetable Pies. 57
Popovers, Yorkshire Pudding. 58

Cookies Brownies & Bars

Ginger Molasses Cookies 60
Outrageous Oatmeal Cookies 61
Chocolate Chip Cookies. 62
Slice and Bake Cookies 62
Awesome Brownies 63
Basic Bar Recipe. 64
Lemon Bars 65
Chocolate Mint Sticks. 66
Maple Bars 67
Rice Krispies Chocolate Bar. 68

Animal Crackers

Doggie Cookies 70
Kitty Treats 71
Pony Cookies 72

Cake

Chocolate Volcano Cake...74

Ginger Cake...75

Lemon or Orange Pound Cake...76

Pineapple Upside-down Cake...77

Perfect Spice Cake...78

Seven Minute Sea Foam Frosting...78

Burnt Sugar Cake...80

German Chocolate Cake...82

Angels from Heaven Cake...84

Sour Cream Chocolate Cake...85

Lemon Poppyseed Cake...87

Carrot Cake...88

Chocolate Ribbon Cake...89

Dessert First

Butterscotch Budino...94

Caramel Apple Cheesecake...95

Authentic New York Cheesecake...98

Brandy Infused Bread Pudding...99

Croissant Bread Pudding...100

Polish Apple Dumplings...101

Baklava...102

Caramel Flan (Baked Custard)...103

Grand Marniere Soufflé...104

Crème Anglaise...105

English Trifle...106

Chocolatte Truffles...107

Pies & Pastries

Basic Pastry Dough...110

Pastry Dough Snacks...110

Meyers Lemon Tarts...111

Apple or Pear Tatin...112

    Pumpkin Pie 114
    French Apple Pie 115
    Shortbread 116

Sauces, Toppings & Fillings
    Pastry Cream 118
    Lemon Curd 119
    Caramel Sauce #1 120
    Caramel Sauce #2 121
    Keto Caramel Sauce 122

Holiday
    Holiday Ornaments 124
    Gingerbread Boys & Girls 125
    Gingerbread People 126
    Gingerbread House 128
    Royal Icing 130
    Spitzbuben 131
    Christmas Plum Pudding 132
    Rum Butter 134
    Cranberry Orange Preserves 135

Gluten Free, Sugar Free
    Almond Paste 138
    Almond Flour Banana Bread 139
    Almond Flour Torte à la GB 140
    Almond Flour Crackers 141
    Almond Flour Oatmeal Cookies 142

    Gingerbread House Plans 143
    Alphabetical List of Recipes 146
    About the Author 149

Dedicated to
Heather MacCurdy
1947–2021
a bestie since the crib

To Be a Baker

When I was a little girl, I played with dolls, wobbled around in my eyelet lace anklets and my mother's high heeled shoes and imagined my future; I wanted to be a nurse. My friend, Heather, and I costumed ourselves à la Florence Nightingale in white full slips, capes made of white terry towels pinned in front with broaches, and our mothers' white lace hankies, which we bobby-pinned to our hair. (We thought they looked like nurses' caps, what can I say?) We wandered the neighborhood, looking for the wounded.

Heather wanted to paint mercurochrome and put band-aids on the fake or sometimes actual wounds. I wanted to give them a donut. Or a piece of warm bread and butter. Or a slice of my mother's apple pie.

I wanted to feed them—wounded birds, friends, parents, brothers. It's about saying I love you, with a donut. Or a pail of soup. A loaf of bread.

I never thought I'd be a professional baker, or own and operate cafes and retreat centers and produce catered food for hundreds. Silly me, I thought I would abandon my dreams and become a housewife in Ohio. I'd marry a Catholic who didn't believe in birth control, and I'd be stuck at home with five kids and a fractious Dalmatian. I'd make five well-balanced lunches every morning at 6, take the little tykes to school and spend my days folding laundry and ironing school uniform shirts while watching General Hospital on my portable TV.

None of those things happened.

Fast forward just a few years, and I am now a retired chef/baker and full-time writer and editor, with a bazillion recipes, having spent my adult life feeding people. I would have been a terrible line cook and, fortunately for me, and the many hungry mouths I fed over the last fifty years, I never spent one moment trying to stay up with a chef flipping burgers my direction for a quick finish of condiments, don't forget the pickle. My biggest fear as a cook was a hotel basement kitchen like Anthony Bourdain's Boiler Room in *Kitchen Confidential.*

My kitchens were studios of nourishment; the dining rooms, salons of sustenance. We focused on harmony in the kitchen, knowing that our own energy and state of mind flow right into the food we prepare.

Not that every kitchen was harmonious, but we did try. Each situation had its might and each its frailty. My career as a chef and baker took me from Rainbow Ranch in Calistoga to the Chopra Center in La Jolla, to Hollywood stars' kitchens and dining rooms to cafes, other retreat centers and even some personal cheffing in ordinary households. My final, and perhaps most dramatic, restaurant experience was Ginna's Café in Carmel Valley, California, where the baked goods were flaky and the snacks I prepared for myself always seemed to end up on the menu.

Now, as David says, GB's Café is wherever I am.

Everywhere, there is dessert. Or toast. Or cookies. People want cake, pie, and savory pasties. This is my collection of over 100 baked items and variations, both sweet and savory. Baking makes me happy, and the recipients, even happier.

Over the years, I have altered many bakery recipes to fit the time, the diet, and the available ingredients. In *GB's Café*, I offer changes such as sugar free, gluten free and just plain improved.

Thanks to David Gordon for the idea for *GB's Café • the bakery*. I believe the thought emerged over a warm piece of sourdough bread slathered with sweet cream butter.

The author at Ginna's Café
Carmel Valley 2001

A friend of mine recently said, "Hot lunch can save the world." I believe this to be true. Doesn't just the idea of Hot Lunch make you feel good? A bowl of soup. Bread made by someone who loves to bake, sliced warm with soft butter on top. Warm apple pie with a slice of cheddar. Sticky buns.

Bakers save the world, one bun at a time. Bake on!

~ Ginna

Pacific Grove, California

Coming next in 2025: *GB's Café - the menu*

— x —

A note about sugar, flours and alternatives

My personal tastes and diet have changed. Sugar is off my A list of foods, but I keep it on hand for the hummingbird feeder. Almost all these recipes can be exchanged for monk fruit one to one for the sugar. It's more expensive than sugar, but worth it. But, remember that monk fruit needs heat to dissolve. Best way I know how to deal with this is to mix the monk fruit with a small amount of boiling water.

And, I have discovered that my various aches and pains of senior adulthood go away when I do not eat baked goods made with mainstream white flour. I use Einkorn and other Italian or ancient flours

Lots of yummy things can be made with almond flour. I play with cassava, etc., but I find that baking with fake flours does nothing but create fake tasting products, bread-shaped cardboard. If you can eat flour with no problems, this is the book for you. If you want to make some changes, you'll find opportunities herein.

Note:

All temperatures shown in this book are **Fahrenheit**

Breakfast and Brunch

Baked Orange French Toast

Baked Orange French Toast is a big favorite. It goes together the night before. Just slip it out of the fridge and into the oven. Done.

Oven 425°

Spray a sheet pan or jelly roll pan with Pam

Arrange 10 slices bread of choice on the sheet pan

Beat together:
2 cups milk
1 cup orange juice
1 tablespoon vanilla
1 teaspoon cinnamon
6 eggs

Pour over bread.
Carefully turn bread once. Be sure all areas of bread are covered.
Can be soaked overnight in the fridge.
Bake uncovered about 15 minutes per side.
 Serve with warm syrup.
Or fruit. Or yogurt. Or all.

Cottage Cheese Pancakes

This yummy thing was made up one morning by a grandmother I once knew.

1 cup flour
1 cup cottage cheese
6 eggs
3 tablespoons maple syrup

Makes a soft batter.

Pour onto hot griddle.

Turn once. Brown both sides.

Great with powdered sugar or syrup.

Dates with Cheesecake Filling

Split one pound of dates, remove pits and fill with a mixture of softened, good quality cream cheese and vanilla, the fresher the better

Legendary Cream Scones

The most famous item on the Ginna's Cafe Menu. 20 years later, people still stop me on the street to say they miss my scones.

Oven 350°

3½ cups organic, unbleached pastry flour
3½ teaspoons baking powder
½ teaspoon salt
1 tablespoon bakers' superfine sugar
2 sticks (1 cup) unsalted butter, cut in pieces
4 eggs
⅔ cup heavy cream
⅔ cup sour cream

Instructions

Sift dry ingredients.

Beat eggs, cream, and sour cream together in a separate bowl.

Mix dry ingredients and cold butter in food processor until mixture looks and feels like coarse meal, less than a minute.

Add egg and cream mixture and flavor; quickly mix together in food processor until dough forms a soft ball.

Scoop out about one cup of dough for each scone onto sheet pan covered with parchment.

Sprinkle with sugar (optional).

Bake about 20 minutes, or until golden and cooked through.

See the following page for a few flavor options

Cream Scone flavor possibilities:

- 1 cup dried cranberries (any dried fruit), hydrated in warm water for five minutes and drained
- 1 cup raisins with 1 teaspoon cinnamon
- 1 teaspoon lemon zest with 1 tablespoon lemon juice
- 1 cup chopped crystallized ginger
- 1 cup cheddar cheese, ½ cup parmesan cheese, 1 tablespoon each: dried basil, dried thyme, dried oregano (sprinkle with parmesan instead of sugar)

The World's Greatest Pancakes

My father was famous for two things in the kitchen. He was big on breakfast. He said we could have anything we wanted for breakfast, provided it was hot. My favorites were Campbell's Beef and Barley Soup and Hamburgers. My mother's warm apple pie with a slice of melted yellow cheese was also a winner. But his best contribution to the betterment of society, or at least our breakfast table, was this recipe for the World's Greatest Pancakes. He said, "If these cakes don't practically float off the platter, you've done something wrong."

3 eggs
2 cups flour (all purpose, sifted)
2½ cups buttermilk
½ teaspoon salt
1 heaping teaspoon baking powder
1 teaspoon baking soda
1 tablespoon melted butter
1 tablespoon warm syrup

About an hour ahead of time, separate the whites of the eggs from the yolk. Let whites come to room temperature. Return yolks to ice box.

When ready to proceed, put buttermilk in mixing bowl and add the soda. Stir. Put flour in another bowl and add the salt and baking powder. Beat yolks and stir thoroughly into the buttermilk mixture. Stir in the dry ingredients. Stir thoroughly – don't beat. Add butter and syrup. Stir, don't beat.

Preheat griddle to 400° (don't grease griddle). When griddle is ready, beat egg whites until they form soft peaks, then fold whites into rest of mixture. Using a cooking spoon, drop spoonsful of the batter onto the dry griddle, spreading lightly until each pancake is a little larger than a silver dollar (the old kind, he wrote).

Bake until air holes pop open and remain open. Turn once. Serve golden brown. Makes approximately 40 two-inch pancakes.

Granola Two Ways

Low Fat, Sugar Free Granola

Oven 325°

2 cups organic rolled oats
2 tablespoons cinnamon
1 tablespoon cardamom
½ teaspoon salt, optional
2 tablespoons grated orange peel
½ cup apple or orange juice concentrate, thawed or
½ cup melted butter
½ cup date pieces
½ cup raisins or currants
½ cup mixed dried fruit pieces
½ cup coconut, optional

In a large mixing bowl, combine the oats, spices and orange peel.

Add the juice concentrate or melted butter and mix well with large wooden spoon.

Spread mixture on parchment covered baking sheets - bake for about 45 minutes or until lightly toasted and dry.

Cool before adding fruits and optional coconut.

Omit the coconut for less fat.

Not Ordinary Granola

Oven 325°

8 cups quick cooking oats (quick rolled oats make a more delicate product)
1 stick unsalted butter, melted
½ to ¾ cup golden monk fruit, dissolved in the warm butter
1 tablespoon cinnamon

Toss all together in a large bowl. Spread on two sheet pans covered in parchment. Bake for approximately 90 minutes, gently turning every twenty minutes or so. The finished product should be golden brown. Add other ingredients after cooling. Store in glass Jars with lids.

Add-ons:
½ cup date pieces
½ cup raisins or currants
½ cup mixed dried fruit pieces
½ cup coconut, optional

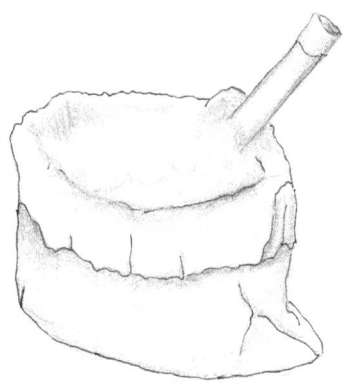

Apple Fritters

2 cups sifted all-purpose flour
½ cup sugar
2 teaspoons salt
3 teaspoons baking powder
⅔ cup milk
2 eggs
2 cups finely chopped apple
1 cup confectioners' sugar, sifted

Sift together the flour, sugar, salt, and baking powder.

Add milk and egg; beat until batter is smooth.

Fold in chopped apple.

Drop by teaspoonful into hot oil about 3 inches deep and fry for 2 to 3 minutes, until golden brown.

Drain well on paper towels and roll in confectioners' or cinnamon sugar while still warm.

Serve plain or with syrup.

Quick Breads and Muffins

At my restaurant, Ginna's Cafe, the morning baked goods were key to a successful day and satisfied customers. My baker, Raymundo, learned all my recipes by heart so he wouldn't be encumbered by a three-ring binder in the tiny kitchen he shared with six other people. We both arrived at 5am to ensure a good start to the day. By the time the first person arrived for his morning coffee, the aromas were enticing. The Buttermilk Muffins were the first items out of the oven.

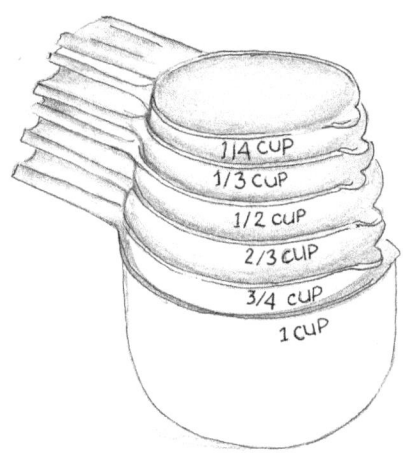

Irish Soda Bread

Soda Bread is a kind of bread-shaped biscuit. Really good with stews or corned beef.

Oven 325°

3 cups all-purpose flour
1 tablespoon baking powder
⅓ cup white sugar
1 teaspoon salt
1 teaspoon baking soda
1 egg, lightly beaten
2 cups buttermilk
¼ cup butter, melted

Grease a 9 x 5 inch loaf pan.

Combine flour, baking powder, sugar, salt, and baking soda. Blend egg and buttermilk together and add all at once to the flour mixture.

Mix just until moistened. Stir in butter. Pour into prepared pan.

Bake for 65 to 70 minutes, or until a toothpick inserted in the bread comes out clean.

Cool on a wire rack.

Wrap in foil for several hours, or overnight, for best flavor.

Cranberry Bread

Oven 350°

1-pound loaf pan, sprayed or buttered
2 cups flour
2 teaspoons baking powder
½ teaspoon baking soda
½ teaspoon salt
¼ cup butter, softened
¾ cup sugar or monk fruit
2 large eggs
1 cup yogurt or buttermilk
Zest of one orange
2 teaspoons vanilla
1 cup whole cranberries, thawed
¼ cup orange juice
2 tablespoons sugar or monk fruit
More orange zest

In a medium bowl, mix flour, baking powder, baking soda and salt.

Cream butter and sugar with an electric mixer for three or four minute, until light and fluffy. Beat in eggs, one at a time, then yogurt or buttermilk, orange zest and vanilla. Turn the speed to low and slowly add the dry ingredients. Don't over mix. Add the cranberries.

Pour into prepared pan. Bake for one hour, or until knife comes out clean.

Meanwhile, stir orange juice and sugar into a bowl. If you are using monk fruit, heat the orange juice first, otherwise the mink fruit will not dissolve.

When bread is done, turn out onto a rack over a sheet of foil or parchment. Poke holes in the warm bread with toothpicks of skewers. Pour the glaze over the bread. Cool completely before cutting.

Cloud Biscuits

Add grated cheddar or parmesan cheese; black olives; dried onion; dried parsley. Try finely diced sun-dried tomatoes; reduce the amount of milk and add a tablespoon of prepared presto; grind up a tablespoon of Indian spices such as turmeric, ginger, cumin, mustard seeds and cinnamon and toss into dry ingredients.

Oven 450°

2 cups all-purpose flour
1 tablespoon sugar
4 teaspoons baking powder
½ teaspoon salt
½ cup softened butter
1 beaten egg
⅔ cup milk*

Sift together dry ingredients. Cut in butter until mixture resembles coarse crumbs.

Combine egg and milk; add to flour mixture all at once. Stir until dough follows fork around bowl.

Turn out onto lightly floured surface. Knead gently with heal of hand about 20 strokes.

Roll dough to a ¾ inch thickness. Dip 2-inch biscuit cutter into flour; cut straight down through dough – no twisting. Place on un-greased or parchment covered baking sheet (¾ inches apart for crusty biscuits, close together for soft sides).

If desired, chill 1–3 hours. Bake 10 to 14 minutes or till golden brown. Makes about two dozen.

*For drop biscuits, increase milk to ¾ cup; omit kneading; drop dough from tablespoon onto baking sheet. Proceed as above.

Date Bread

Oven 300°

One loaf pan or two small loaf pans
Baking spray
2 eggs
2 cups dark brown sugar
⅔ cup neutral oil
1 tablespoon vanilla
2 cups flour
1 tablespoon baking powder
½ teaspoon salt
1 cup buttermilk
1 cup chopped date pieces

Preheat oven to 300°. Blend first four ingredients in KitchenAid or other mixer.

Combine flour, baking soda and salt and add to egg mixture, alternating with buttermilk. Pour into loaf pan.

Add date pieces and stir.

Bake about 30 minutes. Remove from pans to cool.

Delicious with cream cheese.

Prize Winning Blue Cornbread

In the early 2000s, my chef pal, Gayle, and I contributed this cornbread with our turkey chili to the Carmel Valley Chili Cook Off. We won two years in a row, for both the chili and the cornbread.

Oven 350°

1 pound loaf pan
baking spray
1½ cups organic white flour
½ cup blue cornmeal
¼ cup brown sugar
2 teaspoons baking powder
1 teaspoon baking soda
1 teaspoon salt
2 eggs
1 cup buttermilk
¼ cup melted butter

Options: 1 large green onion, chopped
½ bunch cilantro, chopped

Preheat oven. Coat pan with vegetable spray.

Mix flour, cornmeal, sugar, baking powder, baking soda and salt in large bowl.

In another bowl, beat together eggs, buttermilk, and butter.

Mix gently with dry ingredients, folding in ingredients carefully.

Place in prepared pan.

Bake for about 45 minutes, or until inserted skewer or knife comes out clean.

Turn out onto cooling rack and cool slightly before cutting.

Delicious with Ginna's Chili. See the recipe in *The Soup Kit*, page 74.

Buttermilk Muffins

Oven 300°

12 ounce cup muffin pan
Baking spray
2 eggs
2 cups dark brown sugar
⅔ cup neutral oil
1 tablespoon vanilla
2 cups flour
1 tablespoon baking powder
½ teaspoon salt
1 cup buttermilk

Blend first four ingredients in KitchenAid or other mixer.

Combine flour, baking soda and salt and add to egg mixture, alternating with buttermilk.

Pour into muffin cups. Sprinkle with Muffin Topping.

Bake about 30 minutes.

This batter can also be made into individual Bundt cakes. In this case, sprinkle muffin topping into pan, add half the batter, more topping and the rest of the batter. Turn upside down after cooling.

Fruit variations:

Add 2 cups peeled and chopped green apples, or one cup dried fruit hydrated in hot water and drained.

Keep some in your freezer for a rainy day.

Crumb Topping for Muffins & Pies

2 cups organic, unbleached white flour
1 cup cold, unsalted butter
1 cup sugar
1 teaspoon cinnamon

Blend all ingredients in food processor until crumbly, less than a minute. (Do not over blend - will become too doughy.)

Store in airtight container in refrigerator or freezer.

Sprinkle liberally on top of muffin batter or on unbaked pies or apples prepared for baking.

Yeast and Sourdough Breads

My mother introduced me to the art of baking with a yeasted bread recipe. I was three. I stood on a stool at the counter and pressed the rising dough with my pudgy finger. The smell of warm bread means home and hearth to me.

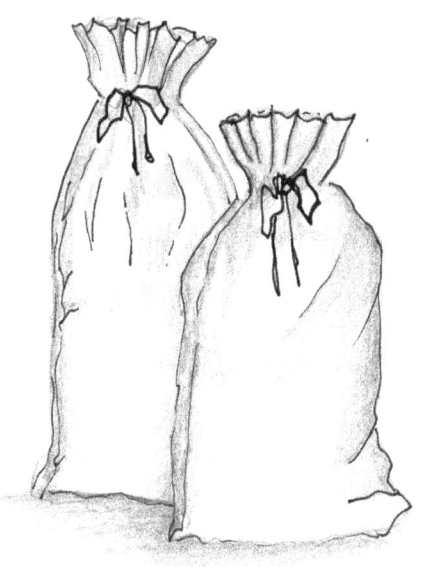

Basic Sourdough Bread

Oven 475°

2 cups white bread flour
¾ teaspoon salt
⅔ cup warm water
⅓ cup white sourdough starter
1 lb. proofing or rising basket or bowl
Proofing linen or clean tea towel
Sheet pan lined with parchment

Mix the four and salt together in a small bowl. (The dry mixture.)

In a larger bowl, place the water and the sourdough starter. (The wet mixture.)

Add the dry to the wet mixture.

Mix with a wooden spoon and then with your floured hands to form a dough, scraping the sides of the bowl clean.

Cover with a towel and let stand for ten minutes.

Leaving the dough in the bowl, pull up a portion from the side and press it into the middle. Turn the bowl slightly and repeat this action eight times. The whole process should take about ten seconds.

Cover the bowl and let stand ten minutes.

Repeat this process twice and the cover for an hour.

Lightly dust your cutting board or clean work surface with flour.

Place the dough on the floured work surface and shape it to fit your basket or bowl. Line the basket or bowl with a floured napkin.

Place the dough in the bowl or basket and cover with the edges of the floured napkin.

Let rise until doubled in size, from three to six hours.

Preheat the oven to 475°.

Place a roasting pan filled with hot water on the bottom rack of your oven. (For a browned bottom on your bread, omit this pan of water,)

Gently tip the risen bread dough out of the bowl or basket onto the sheet pan lined with parchment.

Slide the sheet pan into the oven.

Turn the oven temperature down to 425°.

Bake for about thirty minute or until the top is golden brown.

To check for doneness, tap the bottom of the bread. It should sound hollow.

Cool at least 45 minutes before cutting into it and slathering it with butter and jam.

Sourdough Cinnamon Rolls

Ingredients

8 tablespoons butter, cold
2½ cups all-purpose flour see notes
⅓ cup sourdough starter discard
1 cup buttermilk see notes
1 tablespoon + 1 teaspoon honey or granulated sugar
¾ teaspoon fine sea salt

1 teaspoon baking powder (hold back in initial mix)
½ teaspoon baking soda (hold back in initial mix)

Cinnamon-Sugar Filling

¾ cup light brown sugar
2 teaspoons ground cinnamon
4 tablespoons butter melted

Cinnamon Roll Glaze

1 cup powdered sugar
1 tablespoon butter melted
1 teaspoon vanilla extract
2 tablespoons milk

Equipment

12" Cast Iron Skillet
Mixing Bowls
Bench-Scraper
Cheese Grater
Pastry Brush

Instructions

The night before

Mix the dough: Use a cheese grater to grate the cold butter into a mixing bowl. Add the flour and use a bench scraper or pastry cutter to cut the butter into the flour. Add the sourdough starter discard, buttermilk, honey and salt. Mix with a spatula until the ingredients are well incorporated. Cover the bowl and let rest on the counter for 10-12 hours. (DO NOT add the baking soda or baking powder. This will be added right before rolling out the dough)

The next morning

Make cinnamon sugar filling and glaze: Mix the brown sugar and cinnamon in a small bowl, set aside. In a separate bowl, mix the glaze ingredients and set aside. Preheat oven to 375° and butter a 12" cast iron skillet.

Add leavening agents:

Mix the baking powder and baking soda in a small bowl with a fork until there are no visible lumps. Sprinkle the mixture on top of the dough and mix it in with your hands.

Roll out the dough:

Generously flour your work surface and turn the dough onto it. Flour the top of the dough. Use a rolling pin to roll the dough into a 12" x 22" rectangle.

Cut out rolls: Use a pastry brush to coat the top of the dough with melted butter and sprinkle the cinnamon-sugar mixture evenly over the surface, leaving a half inch bare along the edges. Starting on one side, roll the dough into a log shape. Use the bench-scraper to cut the log into 12 pieces (approximately 1.5 inches). Arrange the portions in the cast iron skillet, leaving space in between each piece to expand.

Bake for 35-40 minutes or until the tops are golden brown. Remove from the oven and glaze while hot.

Notes

In warmer months, the following adjustments will help with a less sticky dough:

Buttermilk: reduce to ¾ cup (180g) of milk.

Flour: Increased from to 2¾ cups (345g) flour.

Measuring:

Use the scoop and level technique to measure your flour if you do not have a kitchen scale. To do this, use a spoon to fluff up the flour in the bag. Use a spoon to scoop the flour into a measuring cup until it is heaped on top. Take a butter knife and level off the top. This should give you the most accurate measurement for flour.

For a lighter cinnamon roll glaze, mix one cup of powdered sugar with a teaspoon of milk. Give it a stir and add a little more milk at a time until you get the consistency you're looking for.

A baking sheet or spring-form pan can be used in place of a cast iron skillet.

Active sourdough starter can be used if desired. Add the salt to the initial mix and skip adding the baking soda and baking powder to the dough. After cutting the cinnamon rolls out, let rise in the skillet for 1-1 1/2 hours at room temperature before baking.

Sample baking schedule

8PM - Mix the butter, flour, sourdough starter/discard, buttermilk, honey and salt in a bowl. Cover and let rest overnight.

8AM - Sprinkle the baking powder and baking soda over the dough and mix in with your hands.

Roll the dough onto a floured surface and brush with melted butter. Sprinkle the cinnamon sugar mixture over the top and roll the dough into a log shape. Cut the log into 12 equal portions and place them in a buttered cast iron skillet.

Preheat oven to 375°

Bake for 35-40 minutes or until golden brown on top.

Remove the sourdough cinnamon rolls from the oven and glaze.

Prep Time: 20 minutes

Cook Time: 35 minutes

Fermenting Time: 10 hours

Total Time: 10 hours 55 minutes

Servings: 12 rolls

English Muffins

1 cup sourdough starter, ripe (fed) or discard; ripe will give you a more vigorous rise
7 cups white flour
½ cup nonfat dry milk
4 tablespoons butter, at room temperature
1 tablespoon salt
Semolina flour or yellow cornmeal, for coating

Combine all the dough ingredients, except the cornmeal/semolina, in a large bowl.

Mix and knead to form a smooth dough. The dough should be soft and elastic, but not particularly sticky; add additional flour if necessary.

Place the dough in a lightly greased bowl, cover, and set aside to rise for about 1½ hours. For more sour flavor, cover the bowl and place it in the refrigerator. Let the dough chill for 24 hours to develop its flavor.

Gently punch down the dough and turn it out onto a lightly floured surface, cover it, and let stand for a few minutes to relax the gluten. Divide the dough in half. Working with one piece at a time, roll ½" thick, and cut in 3" rounds. Re-roll and cut remaining scraps. Repeat with the remaining half of dough.

Or, divide the dough into 24 pieces. Shape each piece into a round ball and flatten into a 3" round.

Place the rounds, evenly spaced, onto cornmeal- or semolina-sprinkled baking sheets (12 per sheet).

Sprinkle with additional cornmeal or semolina, cover with plastic wrap, and let rise until light and puffy, 45 to 60 minutes.

If the dough has been refrigerated overnight, the rise time will be about 2 hours.

Preheat Griddle to 350°

Carefully transfer the rounds to fit without crowding) right-side up to a large preheated electric griddle, or to an ungreased frying pan that has been preheated over medium-low heat.

Cook the muffins for about 10 to 12 minutes on each side, or until an instant-read thermometer inserted in the center of a muffin registers 190°F. The edges may feel a bit soft; that's OK.

Remove the muffins from the griddle, and cool on a rack. Store tightly wrapped at room temperature for 4 or 5 days; freeze for longer storage.

French Bread

2 tablespoons active dry yeast
2 tablespoons sugar
4 cups lukewarm water
8 cups sifted white flour
1 teaspoon salt

In a large bowl, dissolve the yeast and sugar in lukewarm water. Let stand for two minutes. Stir in half the flour and the salt. Add just enough of the remaining flour to hold the dough together – it will form soft, slightly sticky dough.

Knead in the bowl for about five minutes, adding just enough more flour to assist kneading and not stick to your hands. Cover and let rise until double, 1-2 hours. Set near a warm oven or fire to quicken the rising process.

Oven 400°

When the dough has risen, punch it down with your hand and divide into loaves: two medium loaf pans, two baguette pans or one large loaf pan. Clay will produce a great crust. Let rise again for ½ hour to 45 minutes, or until the dough has risen over the top of the pan(s).

Bake for about forty minutes on the middle rack. Place trays of water on the rack below. The loaves will be brown and crusty when they are done. Pierce with skewer for doneness – if they come out clean, that's that!

Oatmeal Bread

Leftover oatmeal? No problem! Makes 2 large or 4 small loaves

Oven 350°

Baking spray

4-5 cups leftover cooked oatmeal or 2 cups raw oatmeal, rolled or steel-cut

4 cups boiling water

8 oz. Dark molasses

2 tablespoons melted butter

1 cup dry milk

3 tablespoons yeast

1 teaspoon salt

4 cups wheat flour

4 cups white flour

Place oatmeal in large mixing bowl, pour boiling water over and stir. Let cool for about two hours or overnight. Dissolve yeast in ¼ cup lukewarm water. To oatmeal, add molasses, melted butter, dry milk, dissolved yeast. Mix well. Let stand fifteen minutes. Add salt and begin adding flour, a little at a time, alternating between wheat and white to achieve a soft but firm dough. You may not need all eight cups flour. Cover bowl and let rise for several hours, until doubled in bulk. Punch down and roll out onto floured board. Knead and shape into loaves. Place dough into well sprayed baking pans and let rise again, until dough comes over top of pans. Bake for approximately 40 minutes. When inserted knife or skewer comes out clean, it's done!

(Cracked wheat or left-over cooked oatmeal can also be used. If using cooked oatmeal, delete the 4 cups boiling water.)

Cinnamon Rolls

Phase one

1 cup lukewarm water

1 tablespoon active dry yeast

2 tablespoons brown sugar or molasses

1/3 cup dry (powdered) milk

1 egg

1½ cups unbleached organic flour, whole wheat or white

Phase two

3 tablespoons melted butter

or vegetable oil

1 teaspoon salt

2½ cups flour

One of the main things I learned about baking bread, from Edward Espe Brown's *Tassajara Bread Book*, is that phase one is about rising, phase 2 adds the salt. If the salt is added in phase 1, it will have a negative, or slowing down affect on the yeast's growth. The sugar feeds the yeast and allows it to fully develop.

In Phase one, the warm water is placed in a warm bowl and sprinkled with the active dry yeast. The sweetener of choice is added, along with the dry milk, which gives a lighter texture, and in the case of sweet bread like cinnamon rolls, an egg. This is then beaten with a spoon, while adding in the first phase of flour. Beat 100 times. Let the "sponge" rise for about an hour before you begin phase two.

Phase two adds the salt, oil or butter and the remaining flour. When enough flour is folded in to begin pulling the dough away from the sides of the pan and the dough no longer feels wet to the touch, it is time to turn it out onto a floured board and begin the hand-over-hand kneading process. This usually takes 10-15 minutes, until the dough is smooth and bounces back to your gentle touch.

Place the dough in an oiled bowl and let rise for about an hour. Punch it down and let rise again.

Phase three

Oven 375*

raisins

cinnamon

melted butter

egg wash (one egg beaten with one tablespoon water)

For Cinnamon Rolls, roll out the risen dough to an approximate 12" x 14" rectangle, about ¼ inch thick. Brush with melted butter and sprinkle with raisins and cinnamon. Roll it up, cut into sections and place flat onto a sheet covered with parchment. Let rise about 20 minutes. Brush with egg wash and bake at 375° for approximately 20 minutes.

Before cooling, you can drizzle the warm rolls with a mixture of one cup powdered sugar and two or three tablespoons orange juice.

Swedish Tea Rings

To make a Swedish Tea Ring, follow the instructions above for Cinnamon Rolls through Phase 2.

Oven 375°

For filling, simmer until thickened (while dough is rising):
1 cup chopped date pieces
and raisins
½ teaspoon cinnamon
1 tablespoon lemon juice
¼ cup brown sugar
⅛ teaspoon salt

Cool completely and spread on the 12" x 14" roll. Roll up as for cinnamon rolls, shape into a circle and place on the parchment covered baking sheet. Cut 1-inch slits into the dough with scissors and twist the roll to expose part of each slice. Bake at 375° for approximately 20 minutes. Before cooling, you can drizzle the warm rolls with a mixture of powdered sugar and orange juice and dot with candied fruit.

Hot Cross Buns

Oven 400°

1 cup scalded milk
½ cup butter, room temperature
½ cup sugar
1 teaspoon salt
1 tablespoon yeast
1 egg, well beaten
About 4 cups sifted white or wheat (or combination) flour
¾ teaspoon cinnamon
¼ teaspoon cardamom
1 cup currants
1 egg
1 tablespoon water

Pour the scalded milk over the butter, sugar and salt; cool to lukewarm.

Add the crumbled yeast and let rest for 5 minutes. Add the egg, cinnamon and cardamom and enough flour to make a soft dough.

Fold in the currants. Let rise in a warm place (80 to 85°) until double - about 2 hours. Cut into about 24 equal pieces and shape into buns.

Place on a buttered baking sheet about an inch apart. Let rise in a warm place until double in bulk — about one hour.

Preheat oven to 400°

Brush tops with the egg slightly beaten with one tablespoon of water. Bake in a preheated oven for 20 minutes. After buns have cooled, decorate top of each bun with a cross.

Golden Crescents

These were my grandfather's favorites, an Americanized version of a French Croissant, which take about ten times as long to make and contain about three times the amount of butter. A Golden Crescent does have the same shape, just not the flakiness. Think: good, quick rolls in a quarter-moon shape.

Oven 400°

Beat with rotary mixer until smooth:
½ cup sugar
½ cup soft butter
1 teaspoon salt
2 eggs
Stir in:
¾ cup lukewarm milk
2 packages yeast (dissolved in the milk)
Mix in with spoon:
4 cups sifted flour

Scrape down dough from sides of bowl. Cover with damp cloth and let rise till double – about 1½ hours. Divide dough into two parts. Roll each into circle about ¼ inch thick and 16 inches diameter.

Cut each circle into 16 pie wedges. Roll up each piece so that the long point winds up on the outside. Stretch each roll gently into crescent shape.

Cover with damp cloth and let rise about one hour.

Bake 10-15 minutes

Brush with soft butter.

Cheese Straws

Oven 375°

½ cup sifted all-purpose flour
Dash salt
2 oz. gruyere cheese, shredded
3 oz. cream cheese
¼ cup butter
1 egg yolk
2 tablespoons water

Sift flour and salt together in mixing bowl.

Cut both kinds of cheese into flour mixture with pastry blender or fork until mixture looks mealy. Then work the dough gently with your hands until it holds together in a mass.

Roll ⅛" thick on a lightly floured surface and cut into thin rectangles about 3" x ½" in size.

Place on baking sheet, brush with mixture of egg yolk and water and sprinkle tops with coarse salt, caraway seeds or poppy seeds.

Bake 10-12 minutes.

Makes lots.

Sour Cream Buns

Heat I cup sour cream to lukewarm in large saucepan*
Remove from heat. Stir until well blended

Add:

2 tablespoons butter

3 tablespoons sugar

I teaspoon salt

Add:

I large egg

I package yeast

Stir until yeast dissolves.

Mix in:

3 cups flour

Turn out onto lightly floured board. Knead lightly a few seconds to form a smooth ball. Cover with damp cloth and let stand ten minutes to tighten up. Roll out dough $1/8$ inch thick into a rectangle 6" x 24". Spread with 2 tablespoons soft butter. Sprinkle with $1/3$ cup brown sugar and one teaspoon cinnamon

Roll up, beginning at wide end. Seal well by pinching edges of dough into roll. Cut into 12 slices about $1\frac{1}{2}$ inch thick. Place in oiled or sprayed muffin cups. Cover with damp cloth and set to rise in a warm place about one hour.

Oven 375°

Bake 12-15 minutes at 375°. While still warm, ice with confectioner's sugar icing.

* To sour sweet cream, measure one tablespoon lemon juice or vinegar into measuring cup. Fill to one cup level with sweet cream

60 Minute Sweet Dough

Heat ½ cup milk to lukewarm in medium sized saucepan
Remove from heat.

Stir in:

1 teaspoon salt

1 tablespoon sugar

1 package dry yeast

Stir until yeast is dissolved.

Mix in:

1 egg

2 tablespoons soft butter

Mix in (just enough to handle easily):

2–2¼ cups sifted white flour

Mix dough with hand in bowl until moderately stiff. Turn onto floured board and knead several times. Shape as directed below.

Cover with damp cloth and let rise in warm place until almost double in bulk – 35-40 minutes.

Oven 400°

Bake 20-25 minutes until golden brown. Serve immediately.

Cinnamon Swirls

Oven 400°

Roll out 60 Minute Sweet Dough into a rectangle 12" x 7". Spread surface with one tablespoon soft butter.

Sprinkle with sugar or brown sugar and cinnamon.

Roll up beginning at wide end. Seal tightly by pinching the edges of dough into roll. Cut into 12 slices.

 cut-side-down with a little space in between in an oiled or sprayed 9 inch round pan or in a circle on a baking sheet.

Bake 20 minutes.

After baking, if desired, mix one cup confectioner's sugar with ⅓ cup orange juice and pour over warm rolls before serving.

Pecan Rolls

Make as for Cinnamon Swirls above – except, place cut sliced in a pan that has been coated with ¼ cup each melted butter, brown sugar and chopped pecans.

When baked, turn pan upside down onto platter.

Glazed Donuts

When we were kids, on Halloween we went country friend to country friend, to bob for apples or just hang out. My mother always brought glazed donuts.

2 packets active dry yeast
1/4 cup lukewarm water
1 1/2 cups lukewarm milk
1/2 cup white sugar
1 teaspoon salt
2 eggs
1/3 butter, softened
5 cups all-purpose flour
1 quart vegetable oil for frying
1/3 cup butter
2 cups powdered sugar
1 1/2 teaspoons vanilla
4 tablespoons hot water or as needed

Sprinkle the yeast into the warm water, and let stand for 5 minutes, or until foamy.

In a large bowl, mix together the yeast mixture, milk, sugar, salt, eggs, butter, and 2 cups of the flour. Mix for a few minutes with a wooden spoon, making a "sponge". Let stand five minutes.

Beat in remaining flour 1/2 cup at a time, until the dough no longer sticks to the bowl. Knead for about 5 minutes, or until smooth and elastic.

Place the dough into a greased bowl, cover and set in a warm place to rise until double.

Turn the dough out onto a floured surface and roll out to 1/2 inch thickness. Cut with a floured donut cutter. Let donuts sit out to rise again until double. Cover loosely with a cloth.

Melt butter in a saucepan over medium heat. Blend in powdered sugar and vanilla until smooth. Remove from heat and stir in hot water one tablespoon at a time until the icing is thin, but not watery. Set aside.

In a deep fryer or heavy skillet heat the oil to 350°. Slip donuts into the hot oil using a wide spatula. Turn donuts over as they rise to the surface.

Fry donuts on each side until golden brown.

Remove from oil and drain on a wire rack.

Dip donuts into the glaze while they are still hot and set on the wire racks placed over a piece of parchment to drain.

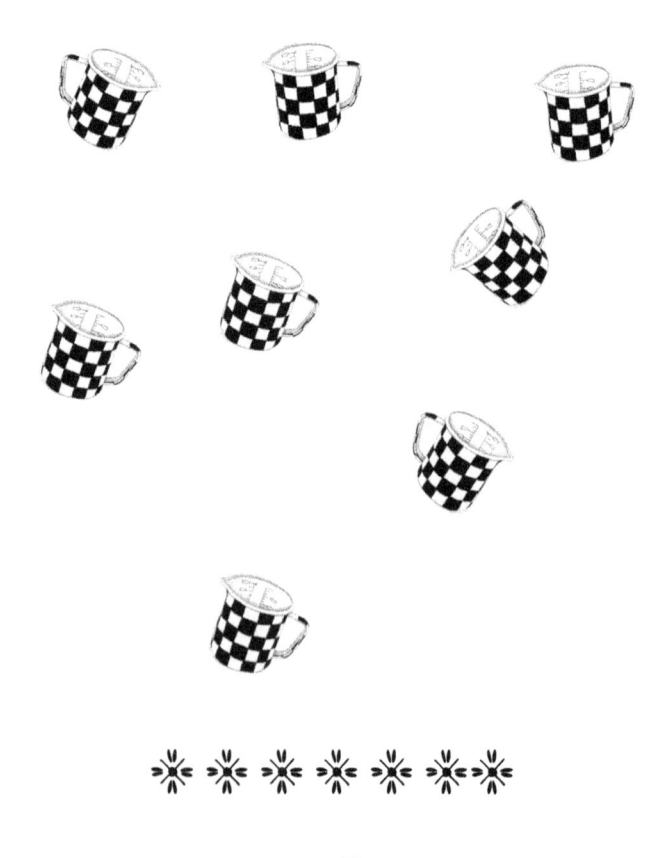

Croissants

Perhaps the most time-consuming recipe in this book, next to the Chocolate Ribbon Cake. It's like making puff pastry—by the time you've finished folding, you'll have 81 layers of butter between 82 layers of dough.

Yeast Preparation

1 teaspoon dry yeast
½ tablespoon sugar
¼ cup lukewarm water

Mix ingredients with the warm water until dissolved, and let sit for 5 min. Active yeast will form soft foamy bubbles on its surface.

Mix one part unbleached all-purpose and two parts unbleached pastry flour.

When measuring cups of flour, skim off the excess with the edge of a knife for consistent quantity. The quantities given here are for 12 croissants. If you are careful with measuring, this recipe can be doubled.

Dough

2 cups of flour mix
1 tablespoon sugar
¾ teaspoon salt
⅓ to ½ cups tepid milk
2 tablespoons neutral vegetable oil

In a mixing bowl, blend the above ingredients and the yeast mix with a spatula, then turn out on the board.

Punch, knead and generally pound the dough, scraping the board often, for about three minutes, until you have a nice, firm, glossy mound of dough.

Place the dough into a bowl and, with kitchen shears, snip across the surface each way to open it to rising process. Cover with plastic wrap, and set aside until it becomes double in bulk. (Rising time depends on the room temperature - faster in summer, slower in winter, as a rule.)

When doubled, punch the dough into a flat circle, wrap it in parchment and chill for about 30 minutes. Chilling makes working with the dough much easier.

Next, take one chilled stick of butter and whack it, roll it and punch it into submission, fast. Don't let it get too soft or melted. Just whack the butter and work it with your hands until it is free of lumps. Put it back in the fridge for a bit if it starts to feel warm. (Don't worry, you'll get the rhythm of it).

Press or roll the prepared dough into a 10-inch circle, and, with your hands, form the butter into a 5" square and center it on the top of the dough. Wash and dry your hands. Gently fold the dough edges over the butter and seal it in by pinching the edges closed.

Flour the rolling pin and both sides of the dough, place it on the floured board with seal side up.

*Begin gently rolling back and forth from the center towards the edges to form a rectangle approximately 15" x 5", pinching the dough over any exposed bit of butter to re-seal it. If the dough becomes too warm, chill it for about 20 minutes and continue. The idea is to evenly spread the butter between the two dough layers, preparing the dough for the next part.

Gently fold the bottom of the rectangle to the center of the dough then fold the top flap over it the same way.

Roll out the dough to the 15" x 5" rectangle and fold and roll again.

Chill the dough before repeating the above from * to end. Leave it folded like a business letter, flour lightly, wrap it in parchment and place it in the fridge for about 2 hours.

When chilled, repeat the above process. You will have 81 layers of butter between 82 layers of dough. Chill again.

Shaping the Croissants

Turn the chilled croissant dough onto a lightly floured board. Roll it into a 20"x 5" rectangle, keeping the edges fairly straight.

Cut in half and chill half of the dough. Roll the one half of the croissant dough into a 12"x 5" rectangle and cut it in thirds and chill ⅔ of the dough.

Roll the remaining ⅓ of it into an approximate 5½" square and cut it in half on the diagonal.

Roll the two triangles out until two sides are 7" in length and the third edge is longer.

Beginning at the long edge, roll up the dough towards the tip of the triangle, then form into a crescent moon with the tip of the triangle on the bottom to keep it from unwrapping during baking.

Place the crescents on a parchment-covered baking sheet about 2" apart to allow for rising.

Form 12 croissants (in a single recipe), and let rest for an hour covered with a plastic wrap. Pre-heat oven to 475°. If desired, freeze the risen croissants for later baking and pop them in the oven frozen.

Glazing and Baking

Oven 475°

Brush the risen (or frozen) croissants with one beaten egg mixed with ½ teaspoon water.

Place in the pre-heated oven and pay attention - they bake quickly - between 10 to 15 minutes depending on the desired color and crispiness.

Savory Flatbreads, Crackers and Pizza

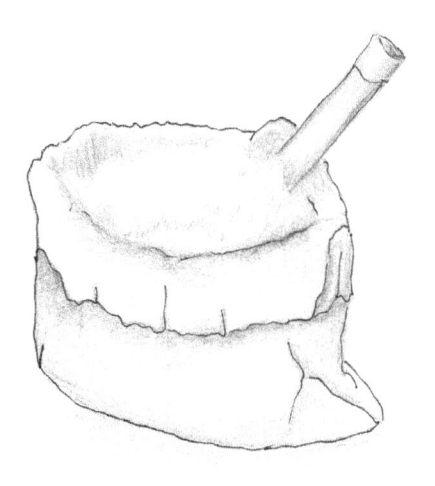

Pizza Dough

Oven 375°

1 cup lukewarm water
1 package active dry yeast
1 tablespoon sugar
2½ to 3 cups flour
2 tablespoons olive oil
½ teaspoon salt

Combine the water, yeast and sugar in a bowl. Let stand ten minutes.

Add half the flour and stir well.

Add the salt and the oil and enough of the remaining flour to form smooth, soft dough. Turn out onto lightly floured board and knead five minutes. If the dough is too sticky, sprinkle with more flour while kneading.

Place dough in a lightly oiled bowl and let stand, covered, about 45 minutes.

After the dough has risen, place on a lightly floured surface and divide into four pieces.

Let stand, covered, 20 minutes. Roll out to desired size. Top with sauce, mozzarella cheese and your favorite toppings.

Bake for about 20 minutes, or until bubbling.

Down Home Corn-Spoon

What can I say? Farm girl.

Oven 375°

3 eggs, separated
1¼ cups milk, scalded
¾ cup corn meal
¾ teaspoon salt
2 tablespoons butter
2 cups fresh corn or
2 cups frozen
or *(dare I say it)* 1 can cream style corn
¾ teaspoon baking powder

Spray a 2 quart shallow baking dish. Stir cornmeal and salt into scaled milk and cook over low heat for a few seconds until the mixture thickens into mush.

Blend in butter and corn. Add eggs and blend in.

Cool.

Beat egg whites until stiff. Fold into cooled egg and corn mixture, adding baking powder, and pour into prepared baking dish.

Bake for about 35 minutes or until golden and puffy.

Serve immediately. Serves six.

Scottish Oat Cakes

Oven 325°

2 cups rolled oats (certified gluten-free)

½ teaspoon baking powder

½ teaspoon fine sea salt

¼ cup unsalted butter, melted (or virgin coconut oil for vegan option)

2 tablespoons honey (use maple syrup or brown rice syrup for vegan option)

½ cup hot (not boiling) water, divided

oat flour for rolling (simply grind more oats)

Line a large rimmed baking sheet with parchment paper

In a food processor, process the oats until coarsely ground. Transfer to a large bowl; stir in the baking powder, and salt.

Stir the melted butter and honey into oat mixture. Stir with a wooden spoon until just blended. Stir in half of the hot water; add more hot water as needed to form a cohesive dough.

Turn dough out onto a floured surface and roll out into a ¼-inch-thickness.

Using a 2½ inch round cookie cutter, cut dough into circles, then transfer to prepared baking sheet. Repeat process with dough scraps.

Bake in preheated oven for 23 to 28 minutes until golden and set at edges. Let cool on sheet on a wire rack for 5 minutes, then transfer to the rack. Serve warm or let cool completely.

Chapatis

Chapatis, tortillas, Asian pancakes…same same. Delicious yeast free, à la minute bread.

Skillet Medium High

2¼ cups flour
  (part whole wheat pastry/white flour
   or all white flour or all whole wheat pastry flour)
2 teaspoons sunflower or other light oil
pinch of sea salt
1¼ cups lukewarm water

Place the flour, salt and oil into the food processor. With the speed on medium, process while slowly adding water. As soon as the dough sticks to itself to form a soft ball, stop adding water. Remove from food processor onto a floured board. Roll in flour and let stand for ten minutes or an hour.

Moisten your hand with oil and make 25–30 small balls, about 1½ inches thick. Roll each ball in flour. Using a rolling pin, roll out balls to form 6 inch circles.

To cook chapatis, heat a large skillet or griddle to medium high. Cook each chapati, either dry or with ghee, for about half a minute each side, until it puffs. Serve immediately or keep covered until ready to serve.

Tortillas

Modern day tortilla making is a snap in the Food Processor.

Skillet Medium High

3 cups unbleached,
organic white flour*
1 teaspoon salt
1 tablespoon neutral oil
¼ to ½ cup water

Place flour, salt and oil in Food Processor. Slowly add water through hole in top while processing. When the dough starts to come away from the sides and form a ball, stop the processor. Scrape dough out of container, dust with flour and place in plastic wrap in the refrigerator for up to 24 hours. Dough can also be frozen and thawed completely before the next step.

Cut dough ball into approximately 12 equal pieces, roll into balls and dust with flour. Set aside. On a floured board, roll each ball into a round, shaping as you go. Tortilla rolling pins are handy - they are small, easy to use, and are curved at either end for easy shaping.

*For Corn Tortillas, substitute masa harina for the flour and use a bit more water. You can leave out the oil. Rolling corn tortillas is easiest between two wet towels or between sheets of parchment. Keep tortillas under a wet towel as you flip them on a hot griddle or in a large frying pan, dry or with a small amount of oil to crisp.

Sourdough Crackers

I made up this recipe during the pandemic lockdown in 2020. Faithfully feeding my sourdough starter, I never discarded the discard. Perfect for crackers.

1 cup Sourdough Starter (Discard) *
2–3 cups flour
1 teaspoon sea salt
½ cup unsalted butter, melted and cooled
2 tablespoons dried herbs of your choice, optional
olive oil for brushing
coarse salt (kosher or sea salt) for sprinkling on top

Equipment needed:
  Small pan for melting butter
  Pastry brush
  Pizza cutter
  Rolling pin
  Parchment **
  1 cup dry measure
  teaspoon
  medium ceramic bowl
  two half-size sheet pans

* *Notes on the Starter*: When feeding a sourdough starter (more info about that in Sourdough Starter), I use the so-called Discard for crackers or bread. So, the feeding process goes like this: Remove one cup Starter from the crock and place it in another bowl. Feed both the Starter and the Discard with one cup flour, one cup water. Blend thoroughly with whisk. Set the original crock of Starter back in its home place and set the bowl with the Discard aside for several hours. Now, it is no longer a Discard, but a part of your cracker dough. Let's just call it the Starter.

Be sure to cover both the crock and the bowl with a light dish towel or cloth. The Starter is ready to be used when there are bubbles forming on the surface – this usually takes about two hours, depending on the weather. You can slow down the process by putting the cloth covered bowl in the fridge and speed up the process by putting the bowl in the sun. I often leave this overnight on the counter and make the cracker dough in the morning.

When it comes time to make the dough, place the salt and about ½ cup of flour in a medium ceramic bowl and slowly add the melted butter, whisking constantly, to form a roux. By doing this, the bowl and the flour absorb any heat from the melted butter before adding the Starter. Blend in the Starter, optional herbs and additional flour as needed to form a soft, sticky dough (Einkorn flour absorbs water more slowly than the conventional versions). Shape the dough into a rectangular slab and dust well with flour. Cover with parchment and place in airtight container and refrigerate for 30 minutes, or overnight.

** *Notes on the Parchment:* I prefer to buy a box of professional parchment (available at food service retailers) which, in my kitchen, lasts about three years. The pieces fit full size sheet pans and, when torn in half, fit half size sheet pans exactly. I prefer professional half size sheet pans to home style baking sheets.

Baking

Oven 300°

Very lightly flour a piece of parchment, your rolling pin, and the top of the dough. Cut the dough into four equal-ish, flat rectangles. Flour those, too.

Working with one piece at a time, roll the dough from the center out to a larger rectangle, enough to fill the parchment, about $1/16$" thick. Remember how you learned to paste paper in grade school? From the center out? Like that. The dough will have ragged, uneven edges; that's OK. Just try to make it as even as possible. The browned edges are fabulous.

Lightly brush with olive oil and sprinkle salt over the top of the dough.

Cut the dough into squares with a pizza wheel or a pastry cutter/scraper thingy.

Prick each square with the tines of a fork. Each rectangle of dough is good for one sheet pan of crackers. Transfer the dough and parchment together onto a sheet pan.

In my cracker kit, I have two sheet pans, so I bake two pans at a time on two racks, one on the right side, one on the left, for best air circulation.

Set your timer at 15 minutes and midway through, rotate the baking sheets: both top to bottom, and front to back; this will help the crackers brown evenly. Bake the crackers for a total of 30 minutes, until the squares start to brown around the edges and no longer soft in the middle. While these two pans are in the oven, roll out the rest of the dough onto the remaining parchment pieces, etc., and set aside.

When browned to your desired color and crispness, remove the crackers from the oven and slide the parchment and crackers off. Slide the second set of cracker dough on parchment onto the sheet pans and repeat oven timing and rotation. Cool completely.

Store airtight at room temperature for up to a week; freeze for longer storage.

Cornish Pasties

A pasty is a turnover, filled with savory meat and or potatoes (Tiddly Oggies), using leftovers, cheese, gravy, veggies, whatever. In the nineteenth century pasties were the lunch of choice, easily slipped into pockets. Make the filling first and let it cool completely while making the Short Crust Pastry.

Filling

1 tablespoon oil
1 onion, chopped
1 carrot, chopped
2 stalks celery, chopped
1 potato, chopped
1 pound ground meat (beef, lamb or chicken)
½ cup stock blended with 1 tablespoon flour
salt and pepper to taste
herbs of choice

Sauté the vegetables in hot oil until tender, about ten minutes.
Add the ground meat and continue cooking until meat is done.
Add stock and flour and herbs of choice and bring to a boil to thicken.
Salt and pepper to taste.
Set aside to cool.

Short Crust Pastry

Oven 400°

2¼ cups flour

¼ teaspoon salt

3 ounces unsalted butter

4 ounces lard (found in most markets
   —you can just use 7 tablespoons of butter instead)

1 egg yolk

3 tablespoons cold water

egg wash, made with a little milk to brush on the tops

Place all ingredients in the food processor and whirl around until it barely holds together to form a soft dough. Knead the dough gently, wrap in plastic and chill for about 30 minutes.

Roll the pastry to a thickness of about ¼ inch. Cut into 6-inch rounds (for four large) or 3-inch rounds (for eight small).

Lay the rounds on a baking sheet covered with parchment and place a mound of filling on one side.

Brush the edges of the pastry with egg wash.

Fold the pastry over the filling to form a half circle. Pinch edges together. Make little steam escape slits in the tops.

Brush with remaining egg wash.

Bake for 30 minutes or until golden.

Serve warm with gravy or room temperature for the lunch box.

Vegetable Pot Pie

Vegetable Filling

2 tablespoons butter
2 cups carrots
3 cups potatoes
6 stalks celery
2 cups broccoli florets

3 T flour
3 cups veggie stock
1 teaspoon tarragon
1 teaspoon oregano
1 teaspoon rosemary
Salt and pepper to taste

1 cup fresh or frozen peas
1 cup fresh or frozen corn

Sauté fresh veggies in the two tablespoons butter until tender. Sprinkle with flour and blend in. Slowly add the stock, gently stirring to keep from forming lumps. Add herbs. Simmer for five minutes until thickened. Add peas and corn. Let cool completely.

Savory Crumb Topping

2 cups white flour
1½ stick unsalted butter, cut in pieces
½ teaspoon salt
2 tablespoons dried parsley

Blend in food processor. Freeze leftover topping in Ziploc bag for later use.

Pastry Dough for Vegetable Pies

Oven 350°

4 cups white flour
½ teaspoon salt
2 sticks unsalted butter,
cut in pieces
1 cup cold water or orange juice

Place flour, butter and salt in food processor and process until mealy.

Slowly add cold juice or water through the top hole in the food processor until the dough comes away from the sides of the container and forms a ball. Use only enough juice or water to bind the dough together.

When the ball of dough forms, stop processing. The less you process dough the better. Dust with flour and refrigerate about thirty minutes. This should make about 12 individual pies or one large pie.

Assembly and baking

When ready to put the pies together, remove dough from fridge and cut into 12 equal pieces (for 12 pies).

Roll out into circles and place in small pie tins with dough extended over the edges, which you will turn under and "flute" along the edges.

Fill with cooled vegetable mixture.

Sprinkle with *Savory Crumb Topping*.

Place pies on a baking sheet covered with parchment and bake for about 35 minutes or until browned and bubbly.

Popovers, Yorkshire Pudding

Popover pan or heavy muffin tin or even a cake pan for one large popover called Yorkshire Pudding

Vegetable spray

6 eggs

1 tablespoon vanilla

½ teaspoon salt

1¾ cups flour

2¼ cups milk (can be whole, 2% or fat free)

4 tablespoon butter, melted

Blend eggs, vanilla and salt in food processor. Add flour and milk alternately while food processor is whirling around. Add melted butter. Pour into pitcher. Cover. Best if refrigerated over night to cure the batter—the popovers will rise higher and pop better.

Oven 375°

Heat popover pan or heavy muffin tin in oven for about fifteen minutes. Quickly remove from oven, spray heavily and pour cold batter to top of cups.

Bake at 375° (without opening the oven door) for about 40 minutes, until dark golden brown and firm to the touch.

Remove from oven and, using bamboo skewer, poke with many holes to allow the steam to escape (otherwise your popovers will collapse).

Serve with butter and jam or maple butter (½ softened butter, ½ maple syrup blended in food processor).

Note: Don't double the recipe. If you want more popovers, make the batter twice.

Cookies, Brownies and Bars

When you need a cookie…

GB's Ginger Molasses Cookies

Oven 325°

parchment for baking
¾ cup brown sugar or monk fruit
½ cup unsalted butter, melted
1 egg
½ cup molasses
2 teaspoons ground ginger
1 teaspoon cinnamon
2 teaspoons baking soda
½ teaspoon salt
2¾ cups organic, unbleached white flour
2 cups chopped crystallized ginger
Bowl of superfine baker's sugar or monk fruit

In a bowl, blend sugar and butter. Add eggs and molasses and blend again. Add remaining ingredients and stir with large wooden spoon or, if you're willing to get your hands into it, mix with hands until a nice gooey mess.

Roll into 2 logs about 2 inches in diameter on a floured board. Sprinkle some flour on two pieces of parchment. Lay the rolled dough onto the parchment and sprinkle with a bit more flour.

Roll up into the parchment and refrigerate for 30 minutes or overnight. If overnight, wrap the rolls in a further layer of cloth, dish towel or plastic wrap.

To bake, cut into ½ inch pieces and roll in remaining sugar. Place one inch apart on parchment covered baking sheet. Bake 8–10 minutes, or just until light cracks appear on the surface. The cookie should be browned on the bottom only.

Outrageous Oatmeal Cookies

Oven 325°

parchment for baking
¾ cup brown or Turbinado sugar
¾ cup unsalted butter, melted
2 eggs
1 tablespoon maple syrup
2 cups organic, unbleached white flour
2 cups rolled oats
1 cup chopped dates
1 cup raisins
1 tablespoon cinnamon
1 teaspoon baking soda
¼ teaspoon salt

Place first four ingredients in large bowl and blend well. Add eggs and blend again. Add remaining ingredients and stir with large wooden spoon or, if you're willing to get your hands into it, mix with hands until a nice gooey mess. Roll into log about 2 inches in diameter on a floured board. Cut into ½ inch pieces and place one inch apart on parchment covered baking sheet. Bake 8–10 minutes, until golden.

Optional Maple Cream Cheese Filling:

1½ sticks unsalted butter, room temp
8oz. cream cheese, softened
3 cups confectioners sugar
1 teaspoon pure vanilla extract
1 teaspoon maple extract, or 2 tbsp Grade B maple syrup (optional)
pinch of salt
Blend in food processor.

GB's Chocolate Chip Cookies

Oven 375°

2¼ cups all-purpose flour
1 teaspoon baking soda
1 teaspoon salt
1 cup (2 sticks) butter, softened
¼ cup granulated sugar
1 cup packed brown sugar
1 teaspoon vanilla extract
2 large eggs
2 cups (12-oz. pkg.) Mini Semi-Sweet Chocolate Morsels
1 cup chopped nuts (optional)

Combine flour, baking soda and salt in small bowl. Beat butter, granulated sugar, brown sugar and vanilla extract in large mixer bowl until creamy. Add eggs, one at a time, beating well after each addition. Gradually beat in flour mixture. Stir in morsels and nuts. Drop by rounded tablespoon onto parchment lined baking sheets.

Bake for 9 to 11 minutes or until golden brown. Cool on baking sheets for 2 minutes; remove to wire racks to cool completely.

Slice and Bake Cookie

Prepare dough as above. Divide in half; wrap in waxed paper. Refrigerate for one hour or until firm. Shape each half into 15-inch log; wrap in wax paper. Refrigerate for 30 minutes.

Oven 375°

Cut into ½-inch-thick slices; place on un-greased baking sheets. Bake for 8 to 10 minutes or until golden brown. Cool on baking sheets for 2 minutes; remove to wire racks to cool completely. Makes about 5 dozen cookies.

GB's Awesome Brownies

Oven 325°

Baking spray
jelly roll or ½ size "hotel" sheet pan
12 ounces bittersweet chocolate
8 ounces butter
8 eggs
3½ cups superfine bakers' sugar
1 teaspoon vanilla
1 teaspoon salt
1 cup flour
1 cup chocolate chips

Melt chocolate and butter in a bowl set over warm water.

In KitchenAid or mixer bowl, beat eggs at medium speed until pale yellow, about three minutes.

Slowly add sugar to egg mixture. Add vanilla and chocolate/butter mixture. Add salt and flour and mix well.

Pour into sprayed jelly roll pan.

Sprinkle with chocolate chips.

Bake about 30 minutes, or until center is firm. Do not over bake.

Cool completely and then cut away edges before serving.

Makes 24 brownies.

Basic Bar

Oven 350°

2 cups organic, unbleached pastry flour
1 cups brown sugar
¼ teaspoon salt
2 sticks cold unsalted butter, cut in pieces

Place all ingredients in food processor. Blend until slightly pasty, almost a pie dough consistency.

Press into the bottom of a baking sheet. Bake fifteen minutes.

Cool slightly before adding topping.

Date Topping

½ cup organic, unbleached pastry flour
1 cups brown sugar
1 teaspoon baking powder
1 teaspoon salt
2 eggs, beaten
2 teaspoons vanilla
2 cups chopped dates*
1 cup pine nuts

Sift first four ingredients in large bowl. Add remaining ingredients and blend well. Spread over cooled crust. Return to oven and bake for twenty minutes, or until golden.

* Variations: replace dates with other dried fruit such as cranberries, apricots, blueberries.

Lemon Bars

Oven 350°

Crust

2 cups white flour
¼ cup turbinado or brown sugar
1 cup (2 sticks) cold, unsalted butter

Topping

3 eggs
½ cup (one stick) unsalted butter, melted
1 cup turbinado or baker's sugar
½ cup lemon juice
Confectioners' for dusting

In a food processor, mix the flour and sugar.

Cut the sold butter into pieces and process with the flour and sugar until it resembles coarse meal.

Press into the bottom of a 9 x 12 baking pan. Bake 15 minutes. Cool slightly.

Combine the topping ingredients in the food processor and blend well.

Pour the topping evenly over the crust.

Bake 25 minutes or until the topping sets. Do not brown.

Cool completely.

Cut into squares. Sprinkle with confectioners' sugar.

Exquisite Chocolate Mint Sticks

Oven 350°

2 sq. (2 oz.) unsweetened chocolate
½ cup butter
2 eggs
1 cup sugar
¼ teaspoon peppermint extract
½ cup sifted all-purpose flour
Dash of salt
½ cup chopped un-blanched almonds.

Grease or spray a 9 inch square glass cake pan. Melt chocolate and butter over hot water. Beat eggs until frothy and stir in sugar, chocolate mixture, peppermint extract. Add flour, salt and almonds. Mix thoroughly. Pour into pan and bake 20 minutes. Cool. Spread top with a thin layer of this filling:

Filling and Glaze

2 tablespoons soft butter
1 cup sifted confectioner's sugar
1 tablespoon cream
¾ teaspoon peppermint extract

Work butter into sugar, cream and peppermint extract. Stir until smooth. Keep filling-covered cake in the refrigerator while you make this simple glaze:
1 sq. (1 oz.) unsweetened chocolate
1 tablespoon butter

Melt chocolate and butter over hot water. Mix thoroughly and dribble over the cool, firm filling. Tilt cake back and forth until glaze covers surface. Refrigerate for at least five minutes.

Cut into strips 2¼ inches long and 3/4 inches wide.

Maple Bars

Oven 350°

Bar

2 cups flour
½ teaspoon baking soda
½ cup light brown sugar or golden monk fruit
½ cup salted butter, softened
1 cup maple syrup
1 large egg
2 teaspoons vanilla

Frosting

½ butter, softened
2 ounces cream cheese, softened
1 tablespoon light brown sugar or golden monk fruit
3 tablespoons maple syrup
¼ cup confectioners' sugar

For the bars:

Lightly grease a 9x9 inch square baking pan

Combine flour and soda in a medium bowl. In a large bowl, beat sugar and butter. Add syrup egg and vanilla. Beat until smooth. Add flour mixture and blend until just combined. Spread out smoothly on top. Bake for 45 minutes or until firm. Cool on rack 10 minutes. Release from pan and cool completely.

For the frosting:

Cream together butter and cream cheese. Add sugar or monk fruit and maple syrup. Beat until smooth. Slowly add confectioners' sugar until thickened. Spread frosting on top of maple bars. Cut into squares or triangles.

Rice Krispies Chocolate Bars

Oven 350 °

3 tablespoons butter
1 bag marshmallows
6 cups Rice Krispies
½ cup chocolate chips

In large saucepan melt butter over low heat. Add marshmallows and stir until completely melted. Remove from heat.

Add Rice Krispies and chocolate chips. Stir until well coated.

Using buttered spatula press mixture into 13 x 9 x 2-inch pan coated with baking spray.

Cool.

Cut into 2-inch squares.

ANIMAL CRACKERS

Crackers and treats for your pets

Doggie Cookies

Oven 325°

parchment for baking
cookie cutter
(dog bone shape is preferable,
although any shape that makes you smile will do)
1 cup rolled oats
⅓ cup butter or oil
1½ cups chicken or veggie stock, brought to boil
¾ cup cornmeal
1 teaspoon sugar
1 cup shredded cheddar cheese
1 egg, beaten
2-3 cups whole wheat flour

Preheat oven. Place parchment on baking sheet.

In a large bowl, combine oats, butter or oil and stock. Let stand 10 minutes. Stir in next five ingredients.

Add 2½ cups of flour, one cup at a time, mixing well after each addition. Turn onto floured board. Knead until no longer sticky, adding flour if necessary. Roll dough out onto floured board to ½ inch thickness.

Cut with cookie cutter and place on sheet one inch apart.

Bake 35–40 minutes or until light brown and dried out (to prevent moisture from turning them into a lovely penicillin blue).

Cool completely before storing in an airtight container.

Kitty Treats

Oven 325°

parchment for baking
dough scraper
1 cup rolled oats
⅓ cup butter or oil
1½ cups fish stock, brought to boil
¾ cup cornmeal
1 teaspoon sugar
1 cup shredded cheddar cheese
1 egg, beaten
2–3 cups whole wheat flour

Preheat oven. Place parchment on baking sheet.

In a large bowl, combine oats, butter or oil and stock. Let stand 10 minutes. Stir in next five ingredients. Add 2½ cups of flour, one cup at a time, mixing well after each addition.

Turn onto floured board. Knead until no longer sticky, adding flour if necessary. Roll dough out onto floured board in long, thin snakes.

Cut with dough scraper (like gnocchi) into little ½ bites and place on sheet.

Bake 25 minutes or until light brown and dried out (to prevent moisture from turning them into a lovely penicillin blue).

Cool completely before storing in an airtight container.

Pony Cookies
At Ginna's Café, these were very popular with the local ponies

Oven 400°

One sheet pan lined with parchment
1 large carrot
1 large apple
1 cup molasses
2½ cups old fashioned oats
1 cup ground alfalfa
2 tablespoons oil

Shred the carrot and the apple in a large bowl. Add the oil, oats, molasses and alfalfa. Stir to combine well.

Drop the treats by tablespoon on to sheet pan covered with parchment. Press down each mound with a fork.

Bake for about 40 minutes or until almost crispy.

Remove from the oven and let cool. Store in airtight container.

Cake

Chocolate Volcano Cake

Oven 350°

12 tablespoons unsalted butter
6 ounces chocolate
3 large egg yolks
3 large eggs
½ cup sugar
1 cup flour
½ cup unsweetened cocoa powder

Place sheet pan in the middle of the preheated oven for 15 minutes.

Combine the butter and chocolate in a bowl or large glass measuring cup over a pot of simmering water. Melt, blend and set aside to cool.

Beat the eggs, yolks and sugar at medium-high for about 5 minutes, until they are thick and pale yellow.

Lowering the speed, gradually add the flour and then the chocolate/butter mixture.

Butter six (6-8 ounce) ramekins and dust with the cocoa. Tap out excess cocoa.

Pour the batter into the ramekins to ⅞ full. Place on the pre-heated sheet tray and bake for 15-18 minutes. The consistency should be firm edges and a soft top. Too runny? More cooking time. To firm, no oozing chocolate? Decrease cooking time. Hard to remove from ramekin? More butter and dusted cocoa.

Let stand on a cool surface for 3 to 5 minutes.

Loosen edges with a paring knife. Invert a dessert plate over each HOT ramekin and carefully invert. Tap the bottom of the plate lightly and lift off the ramekin. Serve with vanilla ice cream or whipped cream.

Ginger Cake

Oven 325°

6 oz. butter, softened
¾ cup brown sugar
4 egg yolks
1 cup dark molasses
2" piece fresh ginger, grated
1 cup crystallized ginger, chopped
⅓ cup yogurt
2 cups flour
½ teaspoon nutmeg
½ teaspoon ground cloves
½ teaspoon ground cinnamon
½ teaspoon ground ginger
1 tablespoon baking soda in 1 tablespoon hot water
4 egg whites

Cream butter and sugar well. Add yolks one at a time. Add molasses, fresh ginger, crystallized ginger and yogurt. Blend well.

Transfer to a large bowl and sift in dry ingredients. Best egg whites until stiff.

While you're beating the egg whites, activate baking soda in hot water. Add this to batter.

Gently fold beaten egg whites into batter ⅓ at a time.

Pour into well sprayed 9x12 inch pan (or a Bundt Pan), spreading batter evenly across.

Bake for approximately 40 minutes.

Serve warm (with whipped cream!)

Lemon or Orange Pound Cake

Oven 350°

3⅓ cups sugar
10 eggs
1 pound butter, softened
Zest of two lemons (or oranges)
3 tablespoons lemon or orange juice
1 tablespoon vanilla
4 cups sifted flour

Place sugar and eggs in Kitchen Aid or other mixer. Set on medium and mix for ten minutes.

Add softened butter and blend well.

Slowly add flour, ⅓ cup at a time, until blended in.

Add remaining ingredients and blend until smooth.

Pour into well sprayed, high sided cake pan, or Bundt pan, and bake covered with foil for 30 minutes.

Uncover and continue baking for 1¼ hours.

Cool.

Pineapple Upside-down Cake

Oven 375°

Iron Skillet
1 can pineapple slices, drained, reserve juice
1 cup brown sugar
1/4 cup unsalted butter
1/2 cup maple syrup
1/2 cup chopped pecans
4 tablespoons unsalted butter
1 cup milk
2 cups organic, unbleached white flour
1 tablespoon baking powder
4 eggs
2 cups sugar
2 tablespoons vanilla

In skillet, reduce juice to heavy syrup. Add brown sugar, butter and maple syrup and melt together. Sprinkle with nuts. Place pineapple slices into skillet on top of mixture. Set aside.

In heavy saucepan, warm milk and butter until butter is just melted. Set aside to cool.

Sift together flour and baking powder. Beat eggs in mixer at high speed until thick ribbons are formed, about seven minutes.

Gradually fold in sugar and vanilla.

Slowly add dry ingredients alternately with cooled milk/butter mixture (this mixture must be cooled so as not to deflate eggs), ending with dry ingredients. Pour over nut mixture in skillet.

Bake for about 40 minutes or until golden and slightly firm.

Cool ten minutes.

Turn upside-down on platter. Makes ten pieces.

Perfect Spice Cake

Oven 350°

2¼ cups sifted cake flour

1 teaspoon baking powder

¾ teaspoon baking soda

1 teaspoon salt

¾ teaspoon cloves

¾ teaspoon cinnamon

Pinch of black pepper

¾ cup butter, softened

¾ cup firmly packed brown sugar

1 cup granulated sugar

1 teaspoon vanilla

3 eggs

1 cup buttermilk

Sift flour, measuring carefully. Sift again with baking powder, baking soda, salt and spices. Sift or roll out any lumps in the brown sugar. Beat in softened butter until it looks like whipped cream. Work in the brown sugar a little at a time. Now work in the regular sugar a little bit at a time. Add vanilla. Continue creaming until the mixture is very fluffy and the grains of sugar almost disappear. This takes a few minutes, but it is key to the Perfect Spice Cake.

When the sugar is all in, add the eggs, one at a time, beating after each addition.

Add flour mixture a little bit at a time, alternating with buttermilk, ending with flour. Pour batter into two sprayed 8" cake pans.

Bake 30–35 minutes, or until cakes edges leave the sides of the pans. Remove from oven.

Allow to rest about five minutes before turning out onto racks to cool thoroughly.

Seven Minute Sea Foam Frosting

2 egg whites, unbeaten
1½ cups firmly packed brown sugar
Dash of salt
⅓ cup water
1 teaspoon vanilla

Cook egg whites, brown sugar and salt in the top of a double boiler, beating constantly about seven minutes, or until frosting stands up in stiff peaks.

Remove from boiling water and add vanilla.

Beat one minute or until thick enough to spread.

Makes enough frosting to cover top and sides of two 8" layers or about 2 dozen cupcakes.

Burnt Sugar Cake

Oven 350°

2 cups sugar
1/3 cup boiling water
2 1/2 cups cake flour
3 teaspoons baking powder
1/2 teaspoon salt
1/2 cup butter
2 eggs
1 cup milk
1 teaspoon vanilla

Place 3/4 cup of the sugar into a heavy-bottomed saucepan over low heat. Stir until melted and a deep brown color. Remove from heat and add water slowly, while stirring. Return to heat and cook about five minutes, constantly stirring. Cool.

Meanwhile, sift flour, then measure and add baking powder and salt and sift again. Cream butter and gradually add remaining sugar, creaming until light and fluffy. Separate eggs. Add yolks, one at a time, to butter sugar mixture and stir well after each addition. Add four tablespoons of the sugar syrup (the rest goes into the frosting) and blend.

Add dry ingredients alternately with milk, about 1/3 at a time, beating after each addition until smooth, ending with flour. Add vanilla.

Beat egg whites until stiff and fold into cake mixture.

Pour batter into two sprayed 9" layer cake pans.

Bake for about 30 minutes.

When cooled completely, cover with burnt sugar frosting.

Burnt Sugar Frosting

1 cup sugar
2 tablespoons water
2 egg whites
2 tablespoons sugar syrup, saved from above
1/8 teaspoon salt
1/2 teaspoon vanilla

Combine sugar, water, egg whites and syrup in the top of a double boiler.

Place over boiling water and, beating continuously, cook for seven minutes, or until frosting is thick.

Remove from heat.

German Chocolate Cake

Oven 350°

Three 9" cake pans, buttered and floured
Baking Spray
1 4-oz. package sweet German chocolate
½ cup boiling water
1 cup butter
2 cups sugar
4 egg yolks
1 teaspoon vanilla
2½ cups cake flour
1 teaspoon baking soda
½ teaspoon salt
1 cup buttermilk
4 stiffly beaten egg whites

Melt chocolate in boiling water.

Cream the butter and sugar until light. (This can be done with your hands – makes a great blend!)

Add egg yolks one at a time, blending well each time.

Add vanilla and melted chocolate and mix well.

Sift flour with soda and salt.

To the chocolate mixture, add sifted dry ingredients alternately with buttermilk. Don't beat hard – just mix well.

Fold in beaten egg whites. Spread batter evenly between three buttered and floured cake pans.

Bake for 35–40 minutes. Cool.

Frosting

1 cup half and half
1 cup Bakers' Fine sugar
3 egg yolks
¼ pound softened butter
1 teaspoon vanilla

Place all ingredients in a saucepan and cook over medium heat for about fifteen minutes, stirring constantly, until thickened.

Add one cup coconut and one cup chopped pecans.

Beat with wooden spoon until of spreading consistency.

Let cool a few minutes.

Spread between layers and on top (not the sides) of cake.

Angels from Heaven Cake

Oven 375°

1 cup cake flour
¾ cup sugar + 2 tablespoons sugar
Whites of 12 large eggs
1½ teaspoons cream of tartar
¼ teaspoon salt
¾ cup sugar
1½ teaspoons vanilla

Angel Food cake pan

Sift cake flour and ¾ cup + 2 tablespoons sugar; set aside.

Beat egg whites *(be sure to keep all yolks out of the egg whites!)*, cream of tartar and salt until soft peaks are formed.

Slowly add the other ¾ cup of sugar while beating on high until stiff peaks form.

Beating on low, add flour mixture and vanilla slowly, folding in the sides and bottom of the batter as it forms.

Carefully spoon the batter into sprayed Angel Food cake pan.

Slide a knife through the batter to remove air pockets.

Bake 30–35 minutes or until the top springs back when touched lightly with your finger. Cool ten minutes.

Remove the cake from the pan by first running a knife around the edge.

Sour Cream Chocolate Cake

Oven 350°

1 cup baking cocoa
1 cup boiling water
1 cup butter, softened
2½ cups sugar
4 eggs
2 teaspoons vanilla extract
3 cups cake flour
2 teaspoons baking soda
½ teaspoon baking powder
½ teaspoon salt
1 cup sour cream

Dissolve cocoa in water; let stand until cool. In a large mixing bowl, cream butter and sugar until light and fluffy. Add eggs, one at a time, beating well after each. Add vanilla.

Combine the flour, baking soda, baking powder and salt; add to creamed mixture alternately with sour cream, beating well.

Add cocoa mixture; beat well.

Pour into three greased and floured 9-in. round baking pans.

Bake for 30–35 minutes or until a toothpick inserted near the center comes out clean.

Cool for 10 minutes before removing from pans to wire racks to cool completely.

Frosting for Sour Cream Cake

2 cups semisweet chocolate chips
½ cup butter
1 cup sour cream
1 teaspoon vanilla extract
4½ cups confectioners' sugar

In a heavy saucepan, melt chocolate chips and butter over low heat; stir until smooth.

Remove from the heat; cool for 5 minutes.

Place in a large mixing bowl; add sour cream and vanilla; beat until blended.

Add confectioners' sugar; beat until light and fluffy.

Spread between layers and over top and sides of cake.

Lemon Poppyseed Cake

Back in the 50s, this cake might have been made with a yellow cake mix and warm Jello poured over the top. Ho boy.

Oven 325°

6 tablespoons milk
6 large eggs, separated
3 teaspoons vanilla
2 tablespoons poppy seeds
3 cups sifted cake flour
Juice of two lemons
2 tablespoons lemon zest
6 tablespoons powdered sugar
1 cup brown sugar
1½ teaspoon baking powder
½ teaspoon salt
3 sticks unsalted butter, softened

Mix milk, egg yolks and vanilla.

Sift together dry ingredients. Add butter and half of egg mixture to dry ingredients. Beat at high speed for one minute.

Add rest of egg mixture and beat again. Beat egg whites until stiff and fold gently into cake mixture.

Bake in well-sprayed or oiled Bundt pan for 40 minutes or until slight cracks appear in the top.

Let cake rest for about twenty minutes. Carefully remove from pan and place upside down on a serving plate.

Glaze with ½ cup sugar and ½ cup lemon juice, which you have brought to a boil before pouring over cake.

Carrot Cake

Oven 350°

2 cups flour
1¼ teaspoon baking powder
1 teaspoon baking soda
1 teaspoon cinnamon
½ teaspoon salt
2 cups brown sugar
1¼ cup neutral oil
4 eggs, beaten
3 cups carrots, grated

Sift together dry ingredients. Cream together sugar and oil, about two minutes. Slowly add eggs. Blend with dry ingredients. Add grated carrots and blend in. Spray a Bundt pan or baking dish. Pour batter into pan. Bake for approximately 40 minutes.

When cooled, drizzle with a mixture of 2 tablespoons orange juice and about ½ cup powdered sugar, or enough to make a thick frosting. This cake is also fabulous without frosting, or with cream cheese.

Chocolate Ribbon Cake

Very complicated, but worth it

Ingredients for Cake

1½ cups (3 sticks) butter, room temperature

2 cups sugar

8 eggs, separated, room temperature

10 ounces bittersweet or semisweet chocolate (do not exceed 61% cacao), melted, lukewarm

1½ cups finely chopped pecans

2 teaspoons vanilla

1 teaspoon ground cinnamon

1 teaspoon ground cloves

1 teaspoon freshly grated nutmeg

1⅓ cups unbleached all-purpose flour, sifted (measured, then sifted)

Pinch of salt

Pinch of cream of tartar

Ingredients for Buttercream

¾ cup sugar

½ cup light corn syrup

4 jumbo egg yolks

1½ cups (3 sticks) butter, cut into small pieces, room temperature

6 ounces bittersweet or semisweet chocolate (do not exceed 61% cacao), melted and cooled (but still pourable)

¼ cup dark rum

Glaze

12 ounces bittersweet or semisweet chocolate (do not exceed 61% cacao), chopped

¾ cup (1½ sticks) unsalted butter, cut into 12 pieces

2 tablespoons honey

¾ teaspoon instant espresso powder or instant coffee powder

Chocolate Ribbons

7 ounces high-quality white chocolate (such as Lindt or Perugina), chopped

½ cup light corn syrup, divided

7 ounces bittersweet or semisweet chocolate (do not exceed 61% cacao), broken into pieces

Cake

Oven 350° Position rack in center of oven and preheat to 350°F. Butter and flour three 9-inch-diameter cake pans with 1½-inch-high sides. Line bottom of each cake pan with waxed paper; butter and flour waxed paper.

Using electric mixer, cream butter in large bowl. Gradually beat in sugar until smooth. Beat in egg yolks one at a time. Blend in melted chocolate. Slowly mix in pecans, vanilla, and spices. Gently fold in flour in 4 batches (batter will be very thick and dense).

Using electric mixer fitted with clean dry beaters, beat egg whites with salt and cream of tartar in another large bowl until medium peaks form. Gently fold ¼ of whites into batter to lighten, then fold in remaining whites. Divide batter among prepared pans, spreading evenly. Bake until toothpick inserted into center of cake comes out clean, 35 to 40 minutes. Run knife around sides of each cake. Let stand 10 minutes. Invert cakes onto racks. Cool to room temperature.

DO AHEAD: Cakes can be made up to 2 weeks ahead. Wrap tightly and freeze.

Buttercream

Stir sugar and corn syrup in heavy medium saucepan over medium heat until sugar dissolves. Increase heat and boil one minute. Meanwhile, using electric mixer, beat egg yolks in medium bowl until pale and thick. Gradually beat in hot sugar syrup; continue beating until mixture is completely cool, about 5 minutes.
Beat in butter one piece at a time, incorporating each piece completely before adding next. Blend in melted chocolate, then rum. (If buttercream looks broken or curdled, place bowl with buttercream over medium heat on stove burner and whisk 5 to 10 seconds to warm mixture slightly, then remove from heat and beat mixture again on medium speed. Repeat warming and beating as many times as needed until buttercream is smooth.)

Reserve ½ cup buttercream. Set one cake layer, flat side up, on rack; spread with half of remaining buttercream. Top with second cake layer; spread with remaining buttercream. Top with third cake layer; use reserved ½ cup buttercream to fill in seam where cake layers meet. Freeze cake until buttercream is firm, about 2 hours.

Glaze

Stir all ingredients in top of double boiler over gently simmering water until mixture is smooth. Remove from over water. Stir until glaze is thickened, about 5 minutes (do not allow glaze to set).

Pour ¾ of the glaze over the top of cake cake. Carefully and quickly tilt cake back and forth so glaze coats sides; smooth sides with spatula, adding some of remaining glaze where necessary. Chill cake until glaze is set.

Chocolate Ribbons

Melt white chocolate in top of double boiler over gently simmering water; stir until smooth. Stir in ¼ cup corn syrup. Pour onto baking sheet. Chill until firm, 30 to 40 minutes. Transfer white chocolate to work surface and knead several minutes.

Shape white chocolate dough into ball. Wrap in plastic. Let white chocolate dough stand at room temperature one hour.

Repeat with bittersweet chocolate and remaining ¼ cup corn syrup.

Cut white chocolate dough into 4 pieces. Flatten one piece into rectangle. Turn pasta machine to widest setting. Run chocolate through 3 times, folding into thirds before each run. Adjust machine to next narrower setting. Run chocolate through machine without folding. If chocolate is more than 1/16 inch thick, run through next narrower setting. Lay chocolate piece on rimless baking sheet. Repeat flattening, folding, and rolling with remaining chocolate pieces. Repeat process with bittersweet chocolate dough.

Cut four 8x1-inch strips from rolled white chocolate dough and four 8 x ½-inch strips from rolled bittersweet chocolate dough. Center bittersweet chocolate strips atop white chocolate strips to form 4 ribbons. Run one ribbon from base of cake to center. Arrange remaining 3 chocolate ribbons equidistant from each other in same fashion so ribbons meet in center (Step 1).

Cut ten 6½x1-inch strips from rolled white chocolate dough and ten 6½x½-inch strips from rolled bittersweet chocolate dough. Center bittersweet chocolate strips atop white chocolate strips to form 10 ribbons. Cut ends off 2 ribbons on diagonal. Starting at center, drape ribbons over top and sides of cake to form trailers. To form loops for bows, fold remaining 8 ribbons in half, layered side out. Cut ends into V shapes (Step 2). Arrange ribbon halves with V shapes at center of cake to form bow (Step 3).

Cut one 3x1-inch strip of white chocolate and one 3x½-inch strip of bittersweet chocolate. Center bittersweet chocolate strip atop white chocolate strip. Fold in ends of chocolate strips and pinch to resemble knot, place in center of bow. Carefully transfer cake to serving platter or cake stand. DO AHEAD Cake can be prepared up to one day ahead. Cover and refrigerate. Bring cake to room temperature before serving.

Dessert First

In 1962 Earl Wilson, in his popular syndicated column, interviewed ballroom dancer and entrepreneur Arthur Murray, who said he always ate dessert first, because life was so uncertain.

Butterscotch Budino

3 tablespoons salted butter

1 cup brown sugar

¼ cup cornstarch

1 cup heavy cream

2 cups whole milk

3 egg yolks

2 teaspoons vanilla or 1 vanilla bean

Salted Caramel:

1 cup sugar

½ cup butter

½ cup heavy cream

¼ teaspoons sea salt (plus more for the top of caramel)

In a heavy-bottomed pot, melt butter over medium heat. Add brown sugar and keep stirring until the brown sugar and butter are completely melted.

Stir in cornstarch. Add heavy cream and whole milk.

Bring to a slow boil and continue to cook and stir until the mixture coats the back of a spoon.

While the milk mixture cooks, place egg yolks in small bowl. To temper egg yolks, spoon a small amount of hot milk into the bowl. Use a whisk and keep stirring. Pour the mixture back into the pot.

Bring back to a boil for one minute. Add vanilla extract or vanilla bean.

Let chill in refrigerator and cool completely. To expedite the cooling process, place in an ice bath.

For Salted Caramel: Melt butter and sugar over medium heat in a heavy-bottomed saucepan. Stir with wooden spoon or heat-resistant spatula until it turns amber colored. Watch that pot! Stir in heavy cream and sea salt. Simmer for one minute.

Caramel Apple Cheesecake

8 whole graham crackers

1 cup lightly toasted walnuts, divided

2 tablespoons light brown sugar

5 tablespoons unsalted butter, melted

½ cup plus 2 tablespoons granulated sugar, divided

1 tablespoon orange zest

3 (8-ounce) packages cream cheese, at room temperature

½ cup plus 2 tablespoons packed light muscovado sugar

4 large eggs, at room temperature

1 large vanilla bean, seeds scraped

1 teaspoon pure vanilla extract

½ teaspoon salt

½ cup heavy cream

1 recipe Apple Mixture, *below*

1 recipe Apple Caramel Sauce, *next page*

Apple Mixture:

2 cups apple juice

¼ cup granulated sugar

1 vanilla bean, reserved from the cheesecake mixture

1 tablespoon cold butter

3 Granny Smith apples, peeled, seeded and thinly sliced

3 Fuji apples, peeled, seeded and thinly sliced

¼ cup apple brandy (recommended: Calvados)

Continued

Apple-Caramel Sauce:

1½ cups granulated sugar
¼ cup water
¾ cup heavy cream
Pinch salt
3 tablespoons apple brandy (recommended: Calvados)
½ teaspoon pure vanilla extract

Crust

Oven 350°

Place the graham crackers, ½ cup of the walnuts and brown sugar in a food processor and process until finely ground. With the motor running, add the butter through the feed tube and process until the mixture just comes together. Spray the bottom and side of the pan with cooking spray. Pat the mixture evenly into the bottom of a 9-inch spring form pan, place on a baking sheet and bake in the oven until lightly golden brown and just set, about 8 minutes. Remove to a baking rack and let cool completely.

Combine ¼ cup of the sugar and the orange zest in a food processor and process until combined.

Place the cream cheese in the bowl of a stand fixer fitted with the paddle attachment and beat until light and fluffy, 3 to 4 minutes. Add the orange sugar, remaining granulated sugar, and light muscovado sugar and beat again until the sugar is incorporated, and the mixture is light and fluffy. Add the eggs, one at a time and mix until just incorporated, scraping the sides and bottom of the bowl. Add the vanilla seeds and vanilla extract and beat until combined. Add the salt and heavy cream and mix until just combined.

Scrape the mixture into the prepared pan. Set the cheesecake pan on a large piece of heavy-duty aluminum foil and fold up the sides around it. Place the cake pan in a large roasting pan. Pour hot tap water into the roasting pan until the water is about halfway up the sides of the cheesecake pan; the foil will keep the water from seeping into the cheesecake. Bake until the sides of the cake are slightly puffed and set, and the center still jiggles, about 55 minutes.

Turn the heat off and prop the door open with a wooden spoon and allow the cake to cook in the water bath for one hour. Remove the cake to a baking rack and allow to cool to room temperature for 2 hours. Cover the cake and refrigerate for at least 4 hours and up to 24 hours until chilled through.

Top with the warm apple topping, drizzle liberally with the caramel sauce and sprinkle with the remaining toasted walnuts. Serve additional sauce on the side.

Apple Mixture:

Bring apple juice, sugar and vanilla bean to a boil in a large sauté pan over high heat and cook until slightly thickened and reduced to ½ cup. Stir in the butter until melted. Add the apples and cook, stirring occasionally, until lightly caramelized and soft. Add the apple brandy and cook until reduced by one half. Transfer the apples to a plate and let cool slightly.

Apple-Caramel Sauce:

Place sugar and water in a medium saucepan and bring to a boil over high heat (do not stir), swirling the pot occasionally to even out the color, until amber in color, 10 to 12 minutes.

While the caramel is cooking. Place the heavy cream in a small pan and bring to a simmer over medium heat. Remove from heat and keep warm.

When the caramel has reached the desired color, slowly whisk in the heavy cream and salt and whisk until smooth. Remove from the heat and stir in the apple brandy and vanilla extract. Keep warm.

Authentic New York Cheesecake

Oven 350°

2½ cups crushed graham crackers

1 stick melted butter

2 tablespoons sugar

24 ounces cream cheese

1 cup sugar

4 egg yolks

¼ cup heavy cream

4 egg whites

¼–½ teaspoon cream of tartar

1 teaspoon vanilla

1 cup sour cream

1 teaspoon vanilla

2 tablespoons sugar

In a bowl, blend together crushed graham crackers, melted butter and sugar.

Beat cream cheese and sugar. Blend in egg yolks and heavy cream. Whip the 4 egg whites and cream of tartar. Add vanilla. Gently fold half into cream cheese mixture, then the other half.

Press graham cracker crust into bottom of large spring-form pan, pressing up sides ½ inch. Gently pour cream cheese mixture into crust.

Bake for 1 hour 15 minutes or until golden brown and cracked on top.

Turn oven up to 425°

Mix sour cream, vanilla and sugar and spread on top of cake.

Put back in oven for 5 minutes.

Chill before serving. Or not. 12 pieces.

Brandy Infused Bread Pudding

Oven 350°

9" cake pan with 4" sides
Baking Spray
6 cups dry bread, cubed into one-inch pieces
1 cup dark brown sugar
1 cup unsalted butter
1 teaspoon cinnamon
1 cup raisins, hydrated in hot water, then drained
½ cup brandy
6 eggs
3 cups heavy cream

Melt sugar and butter together. Place cubes bread into large bowl and toss with the butter and sugar mixture. Add cinnamon and toss again. Set aside.

After draining raisins, add brandy. Beat together eggs and cream. Add both the raisins and the egg and cream mixture to bread cubes and toss again. Set aside for 30 minutes.

Pour into well sprayed cake pan. Cover and bake for 30 minutes. Removes cover and continue baking for an additional 30 minutes or until puffed up, cooked through and browned. Let cool completely before removing from pan.

Serve with Caramel Sauce and whipped cream.

Croissant Bread Pudding

Oven 350°

9" x 12" baking pan
Baking Spray
3 eggs
8 egg yolks
5 cups half & half
1½ cups Bakers' Superfine Sugar
1½ teaspoon vanilla
6 stale croissants
1 cup raisins

Whisk together whole eggs, egg yolks, half & half, sugar and vanilla in a bowl. Set aside.

Slice croissants in half, horizontally. Place the bottom halves of the croissants in the prepared baking dish, add raisins, the tops of the croissants (which traps the raisins inside to prevent them from burning).

Pour the custard over the croissants and soak for 10 minutes, pressing down gently.

Cover the pan with foil and place on a larger pan filled with hot water. Poke foil with holes to allow steam to escape.

Bake 45 minutes.

Uncover and bake an additional 30 minutes, or until custard is set and the pudding is browned.

Cool slightly before serving.

Polish Apple Dumplings with Sherry Sauce

Oven 350°

6 Granny Smith apples, peeled and cored
6 Lemon Pastry Squares, recipe below
½ cup brown sugar
1 teaspoon cinnamon
3 tablespoons butter
1 cup sweet sherry
½ cup water
½ cup sugar

Place each apple on a pastry square.

Mix sugar, cinnamon and butter and spoon into center of apples.

Fold up pastry square around apples and moisten with sherry to seal, making little packets.

Prick outside of pastry packet with fork.

Place about one inch apart on shallow baking pan that has been non-stick sprayed.

Bake about 15 minutes, until the pastry begins to turn golden.

Meanwhile, place sherry, water and sugar in a saucepan and bring to a boil. Simmer 5 minutes.

Pour a little syrup around the apples in the pan.

Bake an additional 15 minutes.

Serve with remaining syrup and whipped cream.

Baklava

Oven 350°

1 pound walnuts or pecans, coarsely chopped
2 ounces sugar
1 teaspoon cinnamon
1 pound phyllo pastry
6 tablespoons unsalted butter, melted
1 cup sugar
1¼ cups water
2 cinnamon sticks
2 teaspoons lemon juice
1 tablespoon lemon peel
2 tablespoons honey (optional)

Mix all filling ingredients in a bowl. Butter base and sides of a 9 x 12 inch baking dish. Cut phyllo to length of baking dish with a sharp knife.

Place each layer of phyllo in buttered pan, brush with melted butter and place evenly around the bottom of the baking dish. After 5 layers of phyllo, spread a thin layer of filling over the Repeat with phyllo and filling, ending with phyllo on the top—4 to 5 layers.

Fold any excess pastry on either of the sides over the filling and brush it all over with butter. Brush the top layer liberally with butter. Trim any excess pastry with a small sharp knife, but remember it shrinks. Sprinkle drops of water all over the top surface and bake for 30 minutes, until golden.

Place all syrup ingredients, except honey, in a saucepan and stir to dissolve sugar. Simmer for 6–8 minutes, add honey and simmer for 5 minutes until it thickens. Pour hot, not boiling syrup slowly all over the baklava (use a strainer) and let it stand to absorb all the syrup. Let cool and cut into pieces.

Caramel Flan (Baked Custard)

Oven 350°

6 small ramekins or a small pie plate
shallow pan for hot water bath
2 cups milk
1 vanilla bean, split lengthwise
6 tablespoons sugar
6 eggs, beaten
1/3 cup sugar

Place the milk and the split vanilla bean into a saucepan and simmer for five minutes set aside to cool. Scrape insides of vanilla bean into the milk before mixing in the 6 tablespoons sugar and beaten eggs.

While the milk is cooling, melt the 1/3 cup sugar – shake, don't stir.

Once the sugar is melted, it will caramelize. At this point, pour it immediately into the ramekins or the pie plate.

Protect your hand with hot pads and tilt to cover the bottom with the caramelized sugar.

Do this quickly, as the sugar will begin to harden.

Pour in the egg mixture. Set the pan with the hot water bath into the oven with just enough water to come up the sides of the chosen container for your custard, and place the container(s) in the bath.

Bake for approximately 25 minutes until just firm and a crack begins to form in the top.

Chill. As the Flan cools, the caramelized sugar will slightly dissolve.

Before serving, loosen the edge of the custard, cover with a plate and invert. The Flan will slip right out, flowing with yummy caramel.

Grand Marnier Soufflé

Oven 400°

6 tablespoons unsalted butter plus additional for buttering ramekins
1 cup sugar plus additional for coating ramekins
¼ cup plus 2 tablespoons all-purpose flour
1 cup whole milk
7 large egg yolks
¼ teaspoon vanilla
⅛ teaspoon orange oil
2 tablespoons Grand Marnier
8 large egg whites

Generously butter eight one-cup ramekins and coat with sugar, knocking out excess.

In a heavy two-quart saucepan, melt butter over moderately low heat and whisk in flour. Cook roux, whisking, 3 minutes. Slowly add milk and cook over moderate heat, whisking, until mixture is very thick and pulls away from sides of pan. Transfer mixture to a bowl and cool 5 minutes. In a large bowl whisk together yolks, vanilla, oil, and a pinch salt, and whisk in milk mixture and Grand Marnier, whisking until smooth. Cool.

In a large bowl with an electric mixer beat whites until they hold soft peaks. Beat in one cup sugar, a little at a time, and beat until it just holds stiff peaks.

Fold one-fourth egg whites into yolk mixture to lighten and then thoroughly fold in remaining whites with a rubber spatula.

Spoon batter into ramekins just to rim and arrange in a large baking pan. Add hot water to reach halfway up sides of ramekins and bake soufflés in middle of oven 20 minutes, or until puffed and tops are golden. Remove pan from oven and transfer ramekins to dessert plates.

Serve soufflés immediately with:

Crème Anglaise

½ cup whole milk
½ cup whipping cream
1 two-inch piece vanilla bean, split
3 large egg yolks
3 tablespoons sugar

Combine milk and cream in heavy saucepan.

Scrape in seeds from vanilla bean; add bean.

Bring milk mixture to simmer.

Remove from heat and remove bean.

Whisk egg yolks and sugar in medium bowl to blend.

Gradually whisk hot milk mixture into yolk mixture.

Return custard to saucepan. Stir over low heat until custard thickens and leaves a coating on the back of the spoon, about 5 minutes (do not boil).

Cover and chill. (Can be made one day ahead.)

English Trifle

One pound cake or sponge cake
1/3 cup sweet sherry or rum
1/2 cup raspberry jam
3 cups mixed berries (sliced strawberries, raspberries, blueberries)
Other fruit, such as bananas or kiwi, sliced

For Custard (or use Crème Anglaise)
8 egg yolks
1 1/4 cups sugar
1 teaspoon vanilla extract
2 cups whole milk
1/2 pint whipping cream
2 tablespoons powdered sugar
strawberries, for garnish

Heat the milk in saucepan over medium low heat.

Beat the eggs with the sugar and vanilla in a double boiler until it forms a ribbon.

Slowly pour the hot milk into the eggs, beating all the time.

Place the mixture in a heavy saucepan and stir over low heat until the custard coats the back of a spoon, 10 to 15 minutes. Don't boil.

Cool completely.

Slice cake into one-inch pieces. Spread with jam. Cut into 1 inch cubes and layer half on the bottom of a glass trifle bowl, or any straight-sided glass bowl.

Sprinkle cake with sherry or rum to soak.

Dot with half the cut fruit, then half the cooled custard.

Repeat. Refrigerate, covered, at least 4 hours.

Whip cream and spread over the trifle. Garnish with strawberries.

Chocolate Truffles

1 cup heavy cream
10 ounces semi or bittersweet chocolate, chopped
5 tablespoons unsalted butter
Scant ¼ cup Grand Marnier or other liqueur
   (Bailey's, Triple Sec, Kahlua)
1 pound bittersweet chocolate
Cocoa and or powdered sugar

Simmer cream in saucepan. When cream comes to a boil, remove from heat and add chopped chocolate and butter. Stir with wire whisk or wooden spoon until thick and smooth. Pour into bowl and continue to beat, adding liqueur of choice. Refrigerate until cool and firm – overnight is best.

When chocolate is firm, shape into one inch balls with scoop or spoon. Place on a parchment covered baking sheet. Makes approximately 36 truffle centers. Freeze.

Melt 1½ pounds of chocolate in top of double boiler. Pour onto parchment covered baking sheet. Gently roll truffle centers through chocolate until coated. Place on clean parchment covered baking sheet. This layer can also be done with white baking chocolate (make sure it's the kind that melts – and spoon it on top of your truffles, to avoid marbling the two chocolates, unless that is your intention). Dust with cocoa or powdered sugar or grated orange peel. Or not. (The recipe can be quadrupled; pour into four plastic one quart containers, add different liqueurs or grounds nuts and raisins, or dried cherries or dates…), then roll in different coatings

Store in airtight container in refrigerator.

For presentation, place Truffles in gold foil candy papers

Pie and Pastries

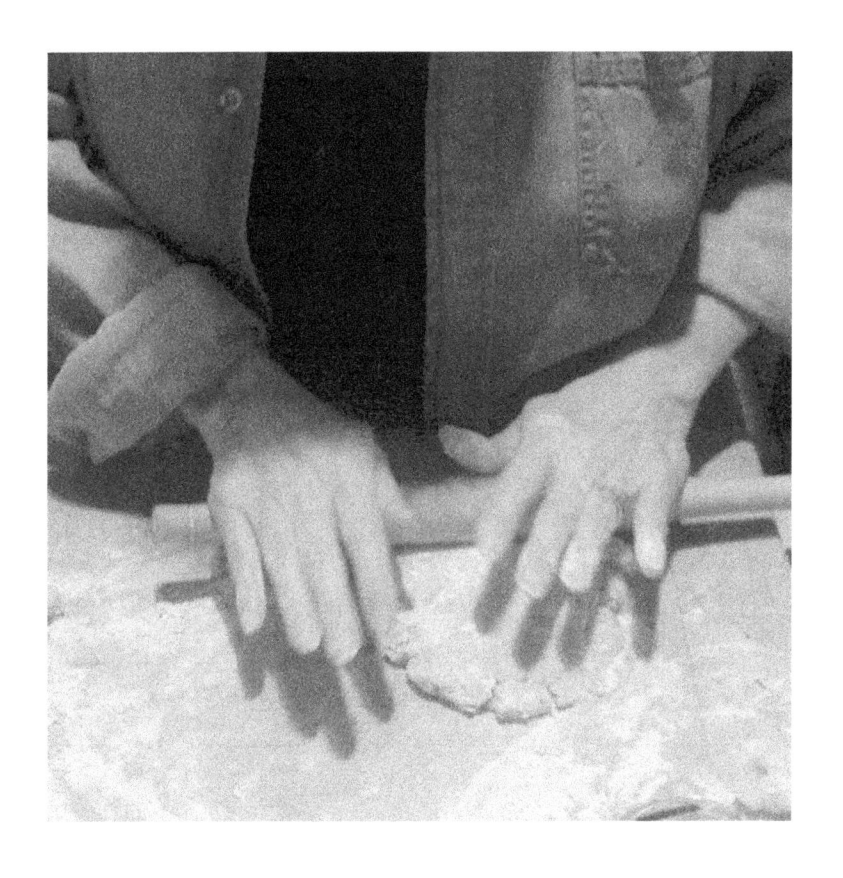

Basic Pastry Dough

For one two-crust pie or two pies with a bottom crust and a crumble topping.

2½ cups pastry flour
1½ cups unsalted butter, cut in pieces
½ teaspoon salt
¼ to ½ cup orange juice

Blend first four ingredients in food processor until butter is distributed and the mixture looks and feels like coarse meal. Slowly add orange juice through top of food processor until a ball of dough begins to form. Do not add too much juice or the dough will be too sticky. Remove from processor, form into a ball, dust with flour, wrap in plastic and refrigerate for one hour or overnight. Roll out onto floured board for pies, pasties or other pastry items.

Pastry Dough Snacks

Cookies

When cutting away the remaining dough around the edges of a pie, set aside on cookie sheets. Spread with soft butter, sprinkle with sugar, cinnamon and a pinch of salt. Bake at 325° for about five minutes.

Kids' Pigs in a Blanket

Wrap extra rolled out pastry dough around a cooked hot dog or sausage and bake it for five minutes.

Turnovers

Fill rolled out pastry dough with several berries sprinkled with sugar and dotted with butter. Roll up and bake about five minutes.

Meyers Lemon Tarts

Oven 350°

One 9" pie tin
One full recipe pastry dough *(opposite page)*
1¼ cup bakers' superfine sugar
⅔ cup sifted cake flour
¼ cup cornstarch
pinch of salt
1½ cups water
5 egg yolks
½ cup lemon juice
2 tablespoons lemon zest

Combine first five ingredients in heavy saucepan. Cook, whisking constantly, until thickened, about ten minutes. Remove from heat.

Add egg yolks, one at a time, whisking each egg in until completely incorporated. Return to heat and stir until thick and smooth.

Add juice and zest. Cool and refrigerate until ready to use.

Roll out pastry dough onto flour covered board.

Place in pie tin. Form flutes around edges.

Place a sheet of parchment in center of dough, add 2 cups dried beans or pastry pearls for baking.

Bake 20 minutes, or until pastry is golden. Cool.

Remove parchment. (Reserve bean for other baking needs).

Fill with cream filling. Refrigerate at least one hour before serving.

Top with additional whipped cream, if desired.

Apple or Pear Tatin

Crust

1 stick butter, cut into pea size pieces
1 cup all-purpose flour, plus extra for rolling
¼ cup sugar
Pinch salt
1 lemon, zested
1 egg yolk
2 to 3 tablespoons ice water

Filling

1 cup sugar
¼ cup apple cider
½ lemon, juiced
1 vanilla bean, seeds scraped
1 stick butter, cut into pats
6 apples, such as Golden Delicious, Granny Smith, McIntosh or your favorite baking apple, peeled, cored and quartered
Mascarpone cheese mixed with 2 tablespoon sugar, for garnish

To make the crust: In a food processor combine the butter, flour, sugar, salt and lemon zest. Pulse until it looks like finely grated Parmigiano. Add the egg yolk and 1 to 2 tablespoons of the water. Pulse, pulse, pulse until the mixture comes together. If it seems a bit dry add a little more water and pulse, pulse, pulse. The mixture should come together into a ball.

Dump the whole thing out onto a clean lightly floured work surface. Knead the mixture one or two times only to make it a smooth ball.

Wrap in plastic.

Refrigerate overnight or a couple of hours.

Assemble and Cook

Oven 425°

To make the filling: While dough is chilling, place the sugar, apple cider, lemon juice, and vanilla bean seeds in a 10-inch nonstick ovenproof pan. Stir to combine. Over high heat bring the mixture to a boil brushing down the sides of the pan occasionally with a pastry brush dipped in water, if necessary. After 6 to 7 minutes the mixture will eventually begin to turn light brown. Swish the pan around gently to promote even cooking. Cook the mixture for another minute or so until the mixture becomes a much deeper amber color.

Remove from the heat and stir in the butter, 2 pats at a time. The mixture will bubble up. That is okay, just be VERY CAREFUL not to get any of this on you.

When all of the butter has been incorporated, begin to arrange the apples rounded side down in circles. Try to do this neatly and in a pretty way. Remember, the bottom will be the top!

Return the pan to the burner and cook over medium for 20 minutes. Remove from the heat.

Retrieve the chilled pastry from the refrigerator. Using a rolling pin or your fingers roll or press the dough out to an even circle about 11 to 12 inches in diameter and place it on top of the apples. Tuck the pastry in around the edges of the pan.

Bake in the preheated oven for 20 to 25 minutes or until the dough is golden brown and crispy.

Let the tart cool for 10 to 15 minutes.

Place a serving platter upside down on top of the pastry and CAREFULLY flip the platter and the pan over.

Let the tart fall gently out of the pan.

Slice tart into individual pieces and garnish with a dollop of sweetened mascarpone.

The Best Pumpkin Pie

Oven 350° with rack in middle

1 cup heavy cream
1½ cups pureed pumpkin
⅔ cup packed light brown sugar
2 large eggs
1 teaspoon ground cinnamon
½ teaspoon ground ginger
¼ teaspoon salt
9" pie or tart pan; pie weights or dried beans
Parchment paper

Make pie shell:

Roll out dough into a 15-inch round on a lightly floured surface with a lightly floured rolling pin, fit into pie pan.

Trim excess dough, leaving a ½-inch overhang. Fold overhang in and press to edge of pan so pastry stands slightly above rim.

Chill about 30 minutes, until firm.

Lightly prick bottom of shell all over with a fork, line with parchment and fill with pie weights.

Bake until side is set and edge is pale golden, 25 to 30 minutes.

Carefully remove weights and foil and bake shell until bottom and side are golden, about 15 minutes more.

Cool completely in pan on a rack, about 30 minutes

French Apple Pie

Oven 400°

One 9" pie tin
½ recipe Basic Pastry Dough *(page 110)*
1 cup Muffin Topping
8 granny smith apples, peeled, cored and cut into 1" pieces
1 stick unsalted butter
½ cups dark brown sugar
½ teaspoon salt
2 tablespoons cornstarch mixed with a few drops of water to form a paste
⅓ cup sour cream

Melt butter and sugar in a large skillet. Add apples and toss to coat with butter and sugar mixture. Simmer for about fifteen minutes, until bubbling.

Mix in cornstarch mixture and cook for 30 seconds, until thickened. Pour onto baking sheet to cool.

Add sour cream.

Roll out pastry dough onto flour-covered board.

Place in pie tin. Form flutes around edges.

Fill with apple mixture. Sprinkle with Muffin Topping and bake about 40 minutes or until pastry is golden brown.

Shortbread

Oven 325°

2 cups butter
1 cup packed brown sugar
4½ cups all-purpose flour

Cream together butter and brown sugar.

Add 3 to 3¾ cups flour. Mix well.

Sprinkle board with the remaining flour. Knead for 5 minutes, adding enough flour to form a soft dough.

Roll to ½ inch thickness.

Cut into 3 x 1 inch strips. Prick with fork and place on parchment covered baking sheets.

Bake for 20 to 25 minutes.

Sauces, Toppings and Fillings

Pastry Cream

4 cups milk
1 cup sugar
12 egg yolks
4 tablespoons flour
4 tablespoons cornstarch
2 tablespoons unsalted butter
2 tablespoons vanilla

Combine milk and half the sugar in a saucepan and heat until sugar dissolves.

In a separate bowl, beat the eggs and the remaining sugar until thickened.

Sprinkle the cornstarch and flour into mixture and continue beating until well mixed.

Beat half of the hot milk mixture into egg yolks then return it all to the rest of the milk mixture.

Bring to boil over medium heat, whisking constantly to prevent scorching. The mixture will be quite thick. Add vanilla.

Pour onto sheet pan to cool.

Rub the top with butter to prevent a film from forming.

Place in an airtight container and refrigerate up to five days.

Can be used for cream pies, trifle, parfaits, strawberry shortcake, etc.

Lemon Curd

3 large lemons
½ cup butter
1½ cups sugar
3 egg yolks, beaten

Wash the lemons and zest the rinds.

Squeeze the lemons and strain the juice into the top of a double boiler. Add the zested peel, butter, sugar, and egg yolks.

Cook, stirring constantly, until the butter melts, the sugar dissolves and the curd begins to thicken, about five minutes.

Don't let it boil – this will curdle the eggs.

When the Lemon Curd is thick and creamy, immediately pour into a clean glass jar.

Cover the curd with a towel or plastic wrap to keep a skin from forming, let cool, and then refrigerate.

Curd will last in refrigerator about three weeks.

This makes about three cups.

Author's Note: Meyer Lemons make a delicious Curd. They have thinner, more orangey skins, a cross between a lemon and a tangerine.

Caramel Sauce #1

1½ cups sugar
½ cup water
3 tablespoons unsalted butter
1 cup whipping cream

Stir sugar and ½ cup water in heavy large saucepan over medium-low heat until sugar dissolves.

Increase heat; boil without stirring until syrup turns deep amber, occasionally brushing down sides of pan with pastry brush dipped into water and swirling pan, about 12 minutes.

Remove from heat.

Whisk in butter. Gradually add cream (mixture will bubble vigorously).

Stir over low heat until smooth.

Cool to lukewarm before serving.

Can be made 2 days ahead. Cover and refrigerate. Re-warm over low heat, stirring occasionally.

Makes 1½ cups.

Or......Caramel Sauce #2

2 cups whipping cream
1 cup (packed) dark brown sugar
¼ cup (½ stick) unsalted butter

Bring cream, brown sugar and butter to boil in heavy medium saucepan over medium-high heat, stirring frequently.

Reduce heat to medium-low and simmer sauce until reduced to 1¾ cups, stirring occasionally, about 15 minutes.

Can be made 2 days ahead. Cover and refrigerate. Re-warm over low heat, stirring frequently.)

Makes 1¾ cups

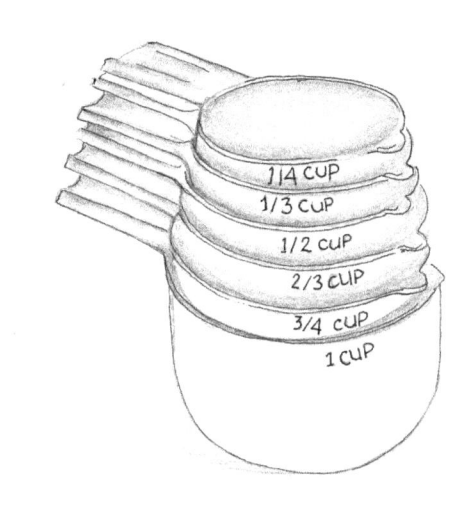

Keto Caramel Sauce

⅓ cup butter
3 tbsp Erythritol (monk fruit)
⅔ cup heavy cream
1 teaspoon vanilla

Melt the butter and sweetener together in a medium-large saucepan over low heat. Once melted, cook for about 3-4 minutes, stirring occasionally, until golden brown. (Watch it carefully to avoid burning.)

Add the cream. Bring to a gentle boil.

Reduce heat to a gentle simmer. Simmer for 7-10 minutes, continuing to stir occasionally, until the mixture is a caramel color and thick enough to coat the back of a spoon.

(If you have a small saucepan, or if you increase the recipe, this can take a lot longer. For example, tripling the recipe can take over 30 minutes at this step.)

Remove from heat.

Whisk in the vanilla extract.

Holiday

Holiday Ornaments

Oven 250°

1 cup salt
2 cups flour
1 cup water
2 tablespoons
vegetable oil
water-based paints

Place dry ingredients in a bowl, add the water and oil, stir until blended. Once the dough holds together, Roll into a ball and kneed it to make a smooth texture.

Place the dough on a cutting-board; roll the dough out a bit thicker than for regular cookies. Cut out the ornaments with cookie cutters or design your own by shaping dough with your fingers.

Don't forget to punch or carve a hole into the top of the ornament for a string to go through to hang the beautiful decoration on your tree!

Bake until hard and dry but not browned—one or two hours. Cool completely and paint with water-based paints or glue on glitter using white household glue.

Thread a string or ribbon through the hole and hang the decoration on the tree

Ornament ideas:

Stars, Hearts, Ducks, Twisted Candy Canes, Trees, Gingerbread Boys & Girls, Big Foot!

Gingerbread Boys & Girls

Oven 350°

4 cups flour
pinch of salt
2 teaspoons ground ginger
1 teaspoon ground allspice
2 teaspoons baking soda
1/2 cup butter
1/3 cup brown sugar
1/4 cup sugar
1/4 cup dark molasses
1 egg, beaten

Prepare sheet pans with baking spray.

Sift dry ingredients into a large bowl.

Cook butter, all the sugars and molasses together in a saucepan until butter melts.

Pour butter mixture into bowl with dry ingredients, add the beaten egg and blend well. Knead lightly to form dough.

Roll out dough to 1/8 inch thickness.

Cut with Gingerbread boy & girl cookie cutters, or pumpkin cookie cutters, or whatever!

Bake about 12 minutes – don't burn the bottoms!

Use glaze icing (sifted powdered sugar and a little water to make a thick icing) for buttons and face.

Gingerbread People *(for a crowd)*
Makes about 6 baking sheets of cookies

1 cup (2 sticks) unsalted butter, room temperature

1 cup packed brown sugar

1 tablespoon ground cinnamon

1 tablespoon ground ginger

½ teaspoon ground cloves

1 cup molasses (not blackstrap)

1 large egg

5 cups all-purpose flour

1 teaspoon baking soda

1 teaspoon salt

For the frosting:

2 cups powdered sugar

¼ cup milk

1 teaspoon vanilla extract

Place the butter, brown sugar, cinnamon, ginger, and cloves in a stand mixer fitted. Beat on medium speed until it resembles thick frosting and no more streaks of butter remain. Scrape down the sides of the bowl, then beat in the molasses followed by the egg until fully incorporated; the dough will be creamy and loose.

Place the flour, baking soda, and salt in a medium bowl and whisk to combine.

With the mixer on low speed, beat in the flour until barely incorporated and just a little flour remains on the sides of the bowl.

Stop the mixer and finish mixing in the remaining flour by hand with a stiff spatula.

At this point, the dough should be very soft and pliable, but workable.

Divide the cookie dough into 3 pieces. Pat each piece into a disk and wrap in plastic wrap. Chill for at least one hour or as long as overnight.

When ready to bake the cookies, arrange 2 racks to divide the oven into thirds and **preheat to 350°**. Line 2 baking sheets with parchment paper.

Sprinkle a work surface lightly with flour. Unwrap one disk of dough and place on top (keep the remaining disks in the refrigerator). Sprinkle the dough and a rolling pin with a little more flour. Roll out the dough to 1/4- to 1/8-inch thick.

Cut out as many cookies as will fit on your baking sheet. Re-roll the scraps and cut out more cookies if the dough is still cool; otherwise pat the scarps into a disk and refrigerate. Continue rolling and cutting the cookies until both cookie sheets are full.

Bake, rotating the baking sheets halfway through, until the cookies feel firm at the edges, are puffed in the middle, and are a toasty shade of brown around the edges, 8 to 10 minutes. Cool for 5 minutes, then transfer to wire cooling racks. Continue rolling, cutting, and baking - make sure the baking sheets are completely cooled between batches.

When ready to frost, stir together the powdered sugar, milk, and vanilla extract to form a smooth icing. It should be thick but pourable. Transfer the icing to squeeze bottles using a funnel; if the icing seems too thick to flow through the funnel, try squeezing the bottle to suction the icing into the bottle and start the flow. If the icing still seems too thick, stir in more milk one teaspoon at a time until workable. (Be careful of adding too much liquid; if the icing is too loose, it will puddle instead of forming lines.)

Decorate the gingerbread cookies. Add candies while the frosting is still wet. Let the icing dry for several hours. The cookies can be stacked between sheets of parchment in an airtight container and kept at room temperature.

Gingerbread House

(Plans are on pages 143-145. Scan or copy to enlarge them to suit your needs)

Structure (walls, roof, chimney, trees, etc.)

18 cups flour
18 tablespoons double-acting baking powder
6 teaspoons ground cinnamon
6 teaspoons ground cloves
1½ teaspoons ground nutmeg
1½ teaspoons ground cardamom
1 teaspoon salt
1¾ cups dark molasses
4¾ cups sugar (may be half brown sugar)
¾ cup butter
1 cup fresh lemon juice
3 tablespoons grated lemon peel
3 eggs
3 egg yolks

This recipe makes enough for three small houses.

Cut out Gingerbread House templates in cardboard and make sure they fit together.

Decorations:

gum drops
cinnamon sticks
almonds, blanched or slivered
walnuts
stick cookies
M&Ms
green sprinkles
chocolate stick cookies
Marzipan or Fondant edible clay
for little animals and windowsills
pretzels
Red Hots

…and any other sweet thing that strikes your fancy and looks like it belongs on a Gingerbread House.

PS: Since there is no ginger in the gingerbread recipe, and it is designed to last for years, I do not recommend eating it. It tastes like sawdust, which is good, I guess, for a house.

To Bake

Oven 350°

Line three sheet pans with parchment.

Sift flour, spices, baking powder and salt into a large mixing bowl. Place molasses, brown sugar and butter in saucepan to melt butter and blend. Cool. Add egg and lemon juice and pour into dry ingredients. Mix well to form a soft dough. This dough can rest overnight.

Knead on floured surface and divide into three equal pieces. On floured surface, roll out dough and press into sheet pans. They should be about ¼ inch thick. Bake about twenty minutes, or until firm and golden. Let cool about five minutes.

Royal Icing:

8 egg whites

12 cups sifted powdered sugar

4 teaspoons lemon juice

4 teaspoons Glycerin (keeps the icing white)

Beat egg whites in bowl. Slowly add in, while beating, powdered sugar, lemon juice and Glycerin. Makes a stiff icing. To prevent drying out, keep icing in plastic containers with lids. Working on a cake board, cutting board or piece of wood covered with parchment; use icing to glue house panels and pieces together:

To Assemble

Glue corner supports to insides of front and back panels, 1/4 inch in from the edge. Attach side panels, butting them up to the corner supports.

Spread icing liberally onto one panel at a time. Let set before you begin adding decorations, using sticks to support windows, etc. With icing, attach roof panels. Glue chimney pieces together with icing and attach to roof.

Decorate at will, using cut outs to represent gingerbread men, trees, fences, logs, whatever you can think of.

This is enough Royal Icing to glue together three small Gingerbread Houses. The icing will last for a week or so.

Spitzbuben

Makes 5 dozen German "Jam Cookies."

Oven 350°

1 cup granulated sugar
1 cup plus 3 tablespoons soft butter
2 cups ground almonds
1 teaspoon vanilla
3½ cups sifted all-purpose flour
Raspberry Jam
Bakers Superfine granulated sugar

Mix together sugar, soft butter, nuts and vanilla.

Mix in flour.

Knead dough very well.

On a lightly floured, cloth covered board, roll to ⅛ to ¼ inch thickness.

Cut with simple cutters.

Place on a parchment lined cookie sheet.

Bake about 20 minutes or until lightly browned.

Let cool.

Spread half the cookies with jam. Top with matching cookie.

Dip in Superfine Sugar.

Christmas Plum Pudding

1 cup currants
1 cup golden raisins
1½ cup raisins
1 cup flour
2 cups stale breadcrumbs
1 cup shredded suet
1 cup dark brown sugar
¼ cup chopped almonds
4 beaten eggs
2 tablespoon Guinness
juice of 1 lemon
juice of 1 orange
½ tablespoon allspice
1 tablespoon nutmeg
½ cup rum
2 tablespoons candied fruit peel

Mix all ingredients together in a large bowl and put in one 7-8 cup English pudding bowl or 2 smaller bowls.

Leave at least one inch at the top of bowl so that the pudding has room to expand.

Cover with two sheets of waxed paper and a layer of aluminum foil.

Tie the top tightly around the rim of the basin with string and make a handle so that the pudding can be lifted.

Lower the pudding bowl into a large pan of boiling water with a saucer upturned on the bottom. The pudding bowl should be about ¾ full.

Cover and simmer for at least 7 hours.

Check that the water does not drop below ¾ of the way up. Add hot more water if necessary.

Remove the pudding and store in a cool place.

When planning to serve, boil pudding for two hours in the same way.

Remove the cover and turn the pudding over onto a serving platter.

Just before serving, warm a little brandy or rum in a saucepan pour it over the pudding, and light with a match.

Serve with Rum Butter or Hard Sauce.

Rum Butter

1 pound brown sugar
½ pound butter
1 cup rum
¼ teaspoon grated nutmeg

Melt butter. Do not let boil.

Beat in sugar.

Stir in rum, a tablespoon at a time and then the nutmeg. Place mixture into a serving bowl and use when set.

Sealed in an airtight container, Rum Butter will keep for over a month in the refrigerator, but DO refrigerate it, to prevent the sugar from re-crystalizing.

Hard Sauce

1 cup powdered sugar
⅓ cup butter
2 teaspoons rum (or vanilla)

Using the back of a wooden spoon, cream sugar into butter.

Add rum (or vanilla).

Refrigerate until firm. Serve over hot plum pudding.

Cranberry Orange Preserves

2 cups dried cherries

1 cup fresh cranberries

3 cups brown sugar

¾ cup crystallized ginger, chopped

4 cups oranges, seeded and chopped (rind and all)

2 tablespoons lemon zest

Combine all ingredients in heavy saucepan with about ½ cup water. Bring to boil.

Reduce to simmer and cook about 8 minutes, stirring occasionally.

When cranberries begin to pop, remove from heat.

Cool. Spoon into jars.

Keep refrigerated.

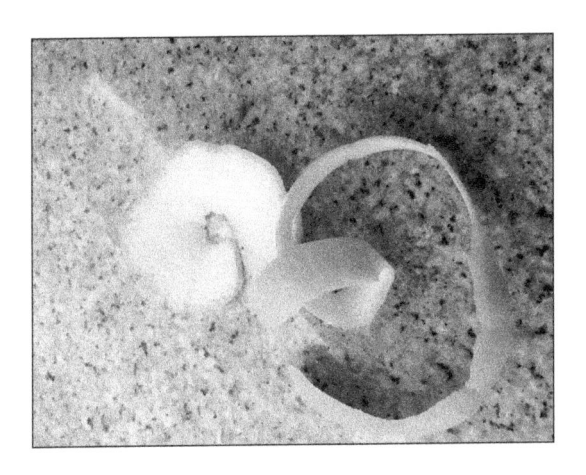

The Gingerbread Farm created in 2011 for the
cover of the cookbook of the same name

Gluten Free, Sugar Free

Almond Paste

1½ cups blanched almonds
1½ cups confectioners' sugar
1 egg white
1½ teaspoons almond extract
¼ teaspoon salt

Blanch whole almonds in boiling water one minute.

Drain and cool. Slip off the skins and discard.

Spread almonds on paper towel or parchment and let dry several hours.

Place almonds in a food processor; cover and process until smooth.

Add the confectioners' sugar, egg white, extract and salt; cover and process until smooth.

Divide almond paste into ½-cup portions; place in airtight containers.

Refrigerate for up to one month or freeze for up to three months.

Yield: 1½ cups.

Almond Flour Banana* Bread

Oven 350°

Butter, oil or spray a one pound loaf pan or two small pans

2¼ cups almond flour
1 teaspoon salt
1 teaspoon baking powder
1 teaspoon baking soda
2 teaspoons stevia
3 eggs, separated
1 cup mashed ripe bananas
1 tablespoon cinnamon
2 tablespoon ghee

Make sure all ingredients are room temperature before you start. Best to keep almond flour in fridge or freezer til about two hours before you are ready to use it.

Combine dry ingredients in a large mixing bowl. Separate the eggs and add the yolks to the banana-cinnamon mixture. Beat the egg whites until stiff.

Slowly add the banana Mash to the dry ingredients. Fold in beaten egg whites. Carefully pour into prepared bread pan.

Bake for approximately 40 minutes, or until browned on top and firm to the touch.

Cool on rack.

Slice the bread and keep in fridge or freezer for longer shelf life

* The mash can be made with roasted squash, cooked zucchini, sautéed apples. Other things to add are raisins, dates, any dried fruit pieces, really, pine nuts, parmesan. You can go sweet or savory.

Almond Flour Torte

A slightly altered recipe from my friend, Dana Marie Mitchell, chef and baker extraordinaire

Oven 350°

2 cups almond flour

1 teaspoon baking powder

1 teaspoon sea salt

½ cup (1 stick) unsalted butter, melted

½ cup sugar or monk fruit

¼ cup maple syrup

4 eggs, at room temperature, separated

1 teaspoon cream of tartar

1 teaspoon vanilla extract

¼ to ⅓ cup slivered or sliced almonds

1 cup fresh or thawed frozen fruit (blueberries, cherries)

Spray 9-inch spring form pan with coconut oil and line bottom with parchment.

Add flour, baking powder and salt to bowl - whisk together.

Mix together melted butter with allulose and maple syrup. Add egg yolks, one at a time, blending each one fully. Add vanilla extract.

Beat egg whites and cream of tartar until soft peaks form.

Add half of flour mixture to egg yolk mixture and beat well. Add remaining flour mixture. Fold in egg whites. Fold gently into prepared pan. Sprinkle fruit onto top and place almond slices around the edges.

Bake until a tester inserted in center comes out clean, about 45 minutes. Let cool in pan for 30 minutes. Un-mold and let cool completely on a wire rack. Transfer to a cake plate.

Slice and serve with whipped cream, crème fraiche or a good quality yogurt.

Almond Flour Crackers

Oven 350°

1 cup almond flour

3 tablespoons sesame seeds

1/4 teaspoon baking soda

1/4 teaspoon salt

1/8 teaspoon pepper

1 large egg, beaten

salt and pepper to top the crackers

Preheat the oven and move the rack to the middle position. Cut two pieces of parchment to fit a large sheet pan. Mine is 18 by 13 inches (46 by 33 cm).

Into a medium bowl, measure and mix all of the dry ingredients. Add the egg and work the egg into the ingredients to form a dough. Divide the dough in half.

Place a piece of parchment onto the counter. Spray it with baking spray. Lay one half of the dough in the center of the parchment. Spray the other piece of parchment and lay it spray-side-down onto the piece of dough.

Roll the dough into a large rectangle about 1/8 to 1/16 of an inch thick. Remove the top piece of parchment and cut the dough into 20 pieces with a large sharp knife or a pizza cutter. Leave the cut dough in place. Salt and pepper the crackers. Slide the parchment onto a cookie sheet.

Bake the almond sesame crackers until they brown slightly, 15–20 minutes. (NOTE: ovens vary in temperature and evenness of heat.) Let them cool for a minute before putting them on a cooling rack to cool completely. Break apart when cool.

Repeat the procedure with the other half of the dough.

Store in an airtight container. Makes approximately 40 crackers. One serving size is 10 crackers, or a quarter of the recipe.

Almond Flour Oatmeal Cookies

Oven 350°

1 cup blanched almond four

1 cup quick oats

1 teaspoon cinnamon

2 tablespoons sugar or monk fruit

¼ cup brown sugar or golden monk fruit

½ teaspoon baking powder

½ teaspoon baking soda

¼ teaspoon salt

1 egg

¼ cup melted butter

1 teaspoon vanilla

1–2 tablespoons milk or milk substitute

1 cup raisins

Line a sheet pan with parchment and set aside

Combine dry ingredients in a bowl and mix well. Add the rest of the ingredients except the raisins and mix well. Use the milk or milk substitute if the mixture is too dry. Add raisins.

Scoop out heaping tablespoons of dough and roll out balls. Place the balls of cookie dough onto the sheet pan with parchment and press down gently.

Bake for ten minutes or until the edges of each cookie are golden. Cool on rack.

Can be stored in plastic Ziploc in the freezer up to six months.

Plans for a Gingerbread House

See recipe and directions beginning on page 128

Side Panels and supports

Back

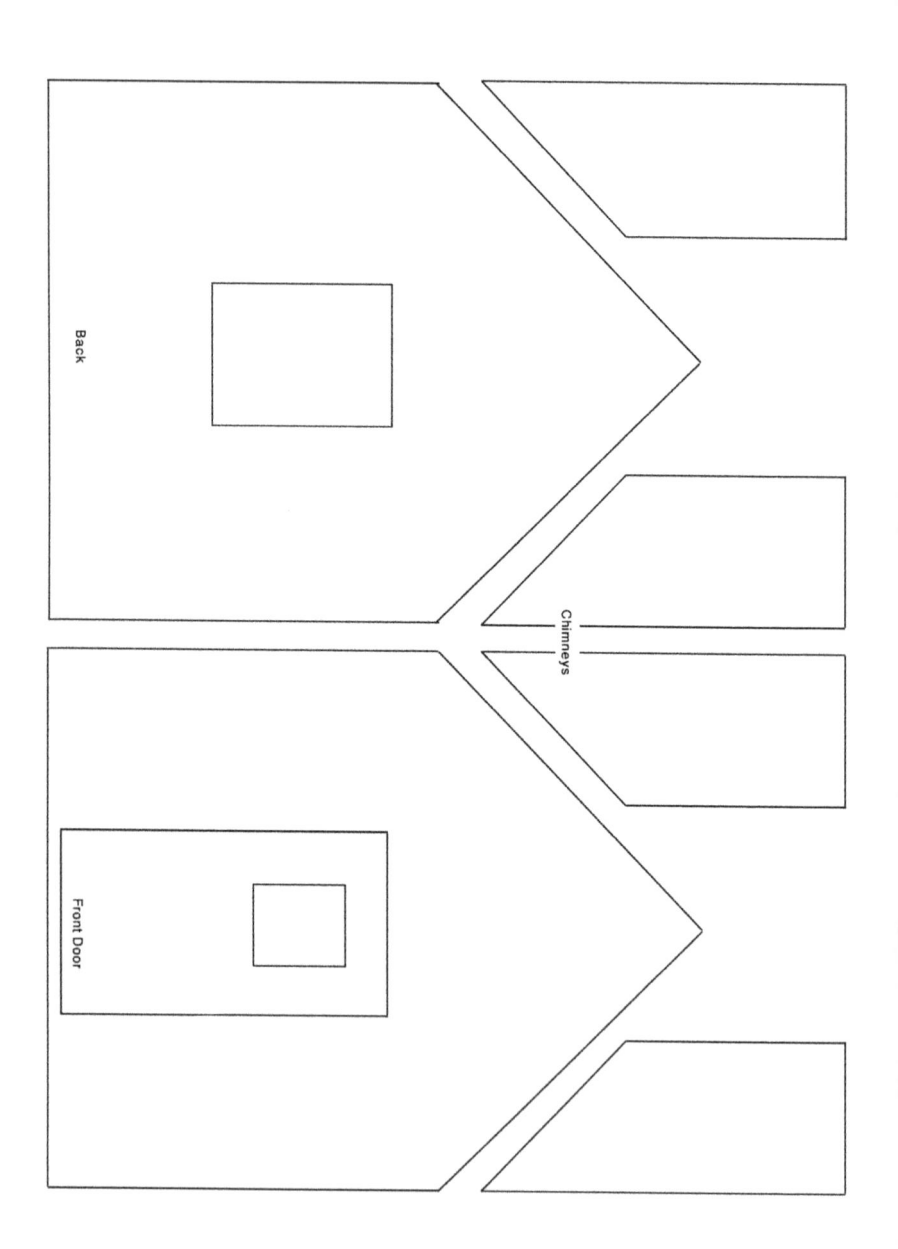

Front Door

Chimneys

Roof Tops

Recipe Index

60 Minute Sweet Dough	37	Cheese Straws	35
Almond Flour Banana Bread	139	Chocolate Chip Cookies	62
Almond Flour Crackers	141	Chocolate Mint Sticks	66
Almond Flour Oatmeal Cookies	142	Chocolate Ribbon Cake	89
Almond Flour Torte à la GB	140	Chocolate Volcano Cake	74
Almond Paste	138	Chocolatte Truffles	107
Angels from Heaven Cake	84	Christmas Plum Pudding	132
Apple Fritters	10	Cinnamon Rolls	30
Apple or Pear Tatin	112	Cinnamon Swirls	38
New York Cheesecake	98	Cloud Biscuits	14
Awesome Brownies	63	Cornish Pasties	54
Baked Orange French Toast	3	Cottage Cheese Pancakes	4
Baklava	102	Cranberry Bread	13
Basic Bar Recipe	64	Cranberry Orange Preserves	135
Basic Pastry Dough	110	Crème Anglaise	105
Basic Sourdough Bread	20	Croissant Bread Pudding	100
Blue Cornbread	16	Croissants	41
Brandy Infused Bread Pudding	99	Crumb Topping	18
Burnt Sugar Cake	80	Date Bread	15
Buttermilk Muffins	17	Dates with Cheesecake Filling	4
Butterscotch Budino	94	Doggie Cookies	70
Caramel Apple Cheesecake	95	Down Home Corn-Spoon	47
Caramel Flan (Baked Custard)	103	English Muffins	26
Caramel Sauce #1	120	English Trifle	106
Caramel Sauce #2	121	French Apple Pie	115
Carrot Cake	88	French Bread	28
Chapatis	49	German Chocolate Cake	82

Ginger Cake	75		Pecan Roll	38
Ginger Molasses Cookies	60		Perfect Spice Cake	78
Gingerbread Boys & Girls	125		Pineapple Upside-down Cake	77
Gingerbread House	128		Pizza Dough	46
Gingerbread House Plans	143		Polish Apple Dumplings	101
Gingerbread People	126		Pony Cookies	72
Glazed Donuts	39		Popovers, Yorkshire Pudding	58
Golden Crescents	34		Pumpkin Pie	114
Grand Marniere Soufflé	104		Rice Krispies Chocolate Bar	68
Granola Two Ways	8		Royal Icing	130
Holiday Ornaments	124		Rum Butter	134
Hot Cross Buns	33		Savory Crumb Topping	57
Irish Soda Bread	12		Scottish Oat Cakes	48
Keto Caramel Sauce	122		Seven Minute Sea Foam Frosting	78
Kitty Treats	71		Shortbread	116
Legendary Cream Scones	5		Shortcrust Pastry	55
Lemon Bars	65		Slice and Bake Cookies	62
Lemon Curd	119		Sour Cream Buns	36
Lemon or Orange Pound Cake	76		Sour Cream Chocolate Cake	85
Lemon Poppyseed Cake	87		Sourdough Cinnamon Rolls	22
Maple Bars	67		Sourdough Crackers	51
Meyers Lemon Tarts	111		Spitzbuben	131
Oatmeal Bread	29		Sugar and Alternatives	xi
Outrageous Oatmeal Cookies	61		Swedish Tea Ring	32
Pastry Cream	118		Tortillas	50
Pastry Dough for Vegetable Pies	57		Vegetable Pot Pie	56
Pastry Dough Snacks	110		World's Greatest Pancakes	7

About the Author

Ginna has owned businesses (Ginna & Co., The Book Studio, Ginna's Café), managed kitchens and cafés in other folks' businesses (Rainbow Ranch Calistoga, the Chopra Center for Well Being La Jolla, The Thunderbird Bookshop & Café Carmel, Cornucopia Café & Market Carmel) and created events for non-profits (Carmel Music Society, the Carmel Bach Festival, the American Tall Ship Institute) as well as for many private clients (including Steven Seagal at his home and on movie sets in Southern California.

Throughout her busy 30-year career in the food and event business, Ginna has entertained herself and friends with art and garden parties, ceramic workshops, gifts from the garden and kitchen and herbal products for the body and table. Ginna is a dedicated Maker, DIY Artist, and Upcycler.

Ginna has authored eleven books. *The Soup Kit* was released in the Fall of 2019. Her cookbooks also include: *A Simple Celebration – the Nutritional Program for the Chopra Center for Well Being* (Random House/Harmony Books 1997); *Bonnebrook Farm* and *The Gingerbread Farm*, memoirs about cooking; and *First You Grow the Pumpkin*, which shares favorite tricks for growing, preserving and creating in the kitchen. *GB's Café: the bakery* is her sixth cookbook.

Ginna studied Ayurveda and its cooking and lifestyle with Drs. Deepak Chopra, David Simon and Shamali Joshi. Her studies in the arts included UCLA Interior Design, the Guild of the Books Arts Carmel, Monterey Peninsula College and privately with myriad artists in and around California, including Alison Stillwell Cameron (Chinese Calligraphy), Tulku Jamyang Rinpoche (Tibetan Thangka Painting) and Louisa Jenkins (collage).

Currently, Ginna and her husband (musician, lecturer and author David Gordon - www.spiritsound.com), are partners in Lucky Valley Press, a pre-press and indie publishing company: www.luckyvalleypress.com. Ginna's cookbooks and novels (*Bear me Away to a Better World*, and *The Lavandula Series*) are available wherever books are sold.

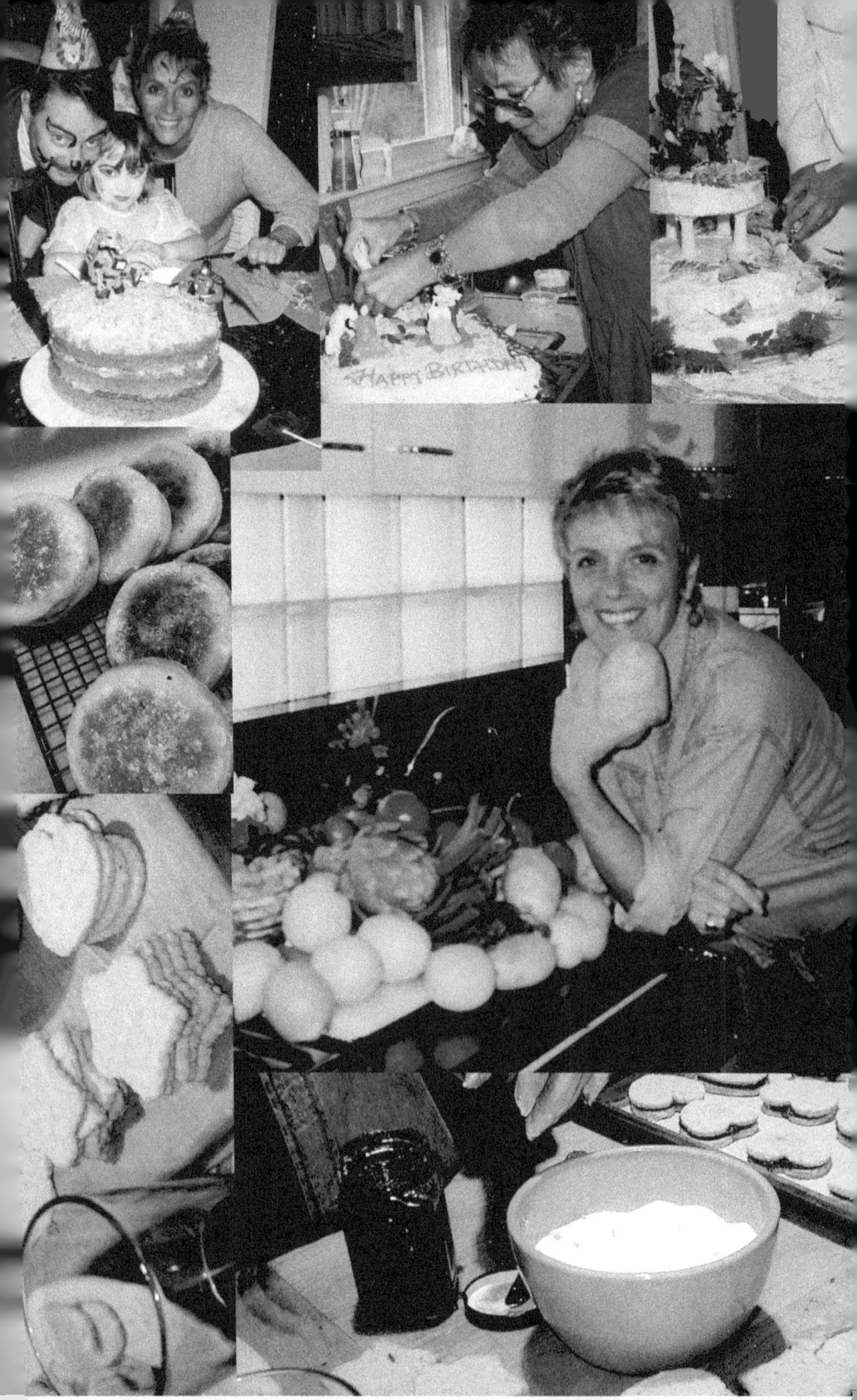

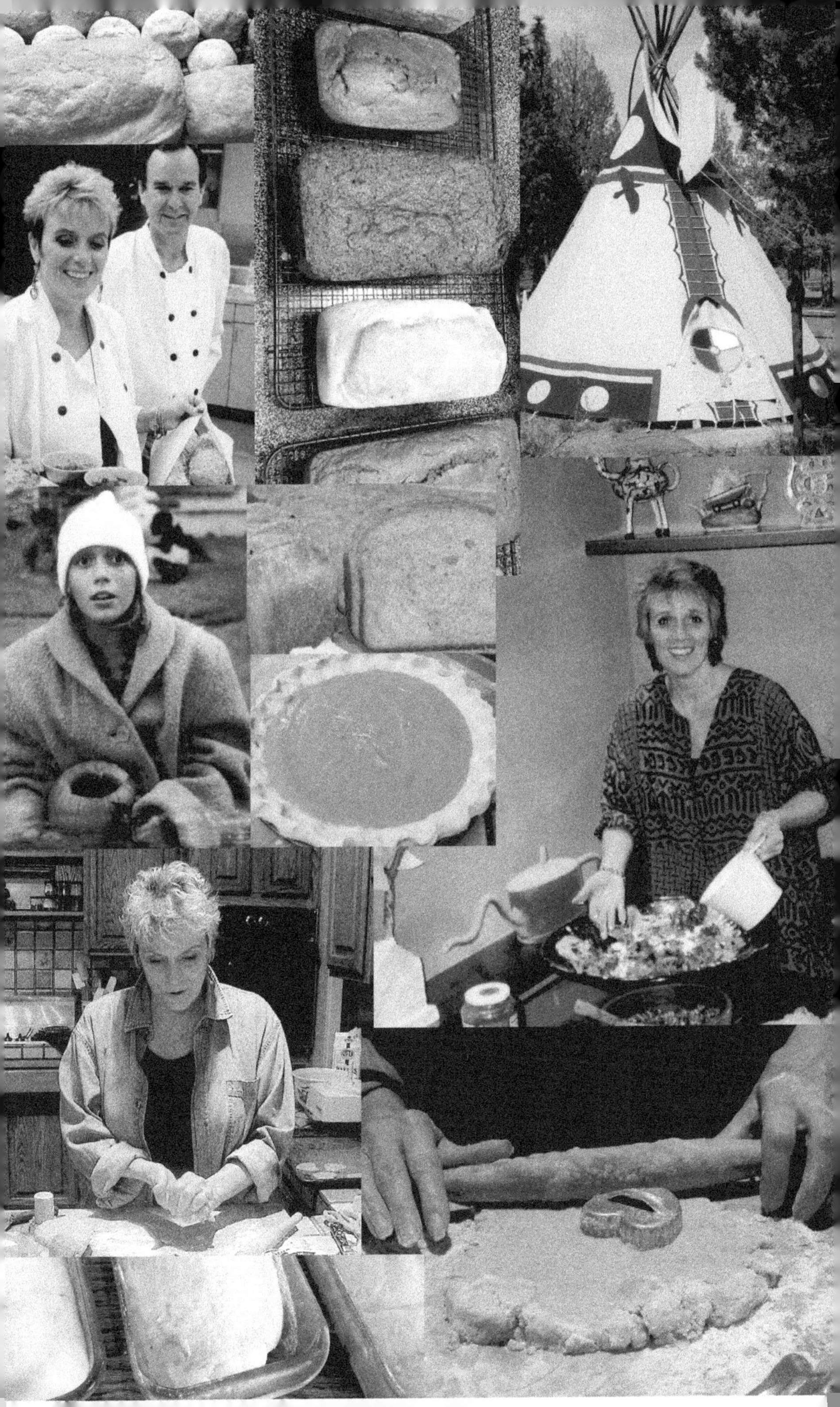